DISCOVERING
CAREERS FOR YOUR FUTURE

government

Ferguson Publishing Company
Chicago, Illinois

Carol Yehling
Editor

Beth Adler, Herman Adler Design Group
Cover design

Carol Yehling
Interior design

Bonnie Needham
Proofreader

Library of Congress Cataloging-in-Publication Data

Discovering careers for your future. Government.
        p. cm.
    Includes index.
    ISBN 0-89434-397-1
1.Civil service positions—United States—Juvenile literature. [1. Civil service positions. 2.Vocational guid-
ance.] I. Ferguson Publishing Company.

JK716 .D585 2001
351.73'023—dc21

                                                                                        2001033081

Published and distributed by
Ferguson Publishing Company
200 West Jackson Boulevard, 7th Floor
Chicago, Illinois 60606
800-306-9941
www.fergpubco.com

Printed in the United States of America
Y-9

Table of Contents

Introduction 1
Ambassadors 6
City Managers 10
Congressional Aides 14
Corrections Officers 18
Customs Officials .22
Deputy U.S. Marshals 26
FBI Agents 30
Fish and Game Wardens 34
Foreign Service Workers 38
Health and Regulatory Inspectors 42
Lobbyists 46
Military Workers 50
Park Rangers 54
Parole Officers 58
Police Officers 62
Regional and Local Officials 66
Secret Service Special Agents 70
Social Workers 74
Spies 78
State and Federal Officials 82
Glossary 86
Index of Job Titles 90
Government on the Web 92

Introduction

You may not have decided yet what you want to be in the future. And you don't have to decide right away. You do know that right now you are interested in government. Do any of the statements below describe you? If so, you may want to begin thinking about what a career in government might mean for you.

___My favorite classes in school are social studies and civics.

___I like to follow political campaigns.

___I participate in student council activities.

___I am interested in police and detective work.

___I like to read books about spies and foreign intrigue.

___I am good at following instructions and keeping rules and regulations.

___I have leadership qualities.

___Knowing I am helping people is important to me.

___I am interested in how laws are made and enforced.

___I am organized and detail-oriented.

___I enjoy reading about political history.

___I have strong feelings about protecting people, property, and my country.

Discovering Careers for Your Future: Government is a book about careers in government, from ambassadors to social workers. Government workers include political leaders who are elected or appointed to their offices. They are also the people who are paid from government funds to protect and help us, such as those in law enforcement and the military.

This book describes many possibilities for future careers in government. Read through it and see how the different careers are connected. For example, if you are interested in politics, you will want to read the chapters on Ambassadors, Lobbyists, Regional and Local Officials, and State and Federal Officials. If you are interested in public service, you will want to read the chapters on Corrections Officers, Military Workers, Parole Officers, Police Officers, and Social Workers. Go ahead and explore!

What do government workers do?

The first section of each chapter begins with a heading such as "What City Managers Do" or "What State and Federal Officials Do." It tells what it's like to work at this job. It describes typical responsibilities and assignments. You will find out about working conditions. Which government workers spend their days in offices? Which ones work in courtrooms, prisons, parklands, or on the street? This section answers all these questions.

How do I become a government worker?

The section called "Education and Training" tells you what schooling you need for employment in each job—a high school diploma, training at a junior college, a college degree, or more. It also talks about on-the-job training that you could expect to receive after you're hired, and whether or not you must complete an apprenticeship program.

How much do government workers earn?

The "Earnings" section gives the average salary figures for the job described in the chapter. These figures give you a general idea of how much money people with this job can make. Keep in mind that many people really earn more or less than the amounts given here because actual salaries depend on many different things, such as the size of the company, the location of the company, and the amount of education, training, and experience you have. Generally, but not always, bigger companies located in major cities pay more than smaller ones in smaller cities and towns, and people with more education, training, and experience earn more. Also remember that these figures are current averages. They will probably be different by the time you are ready to enter the workforce.

What will the future be like for careers in government?

The "Outlook" section discusses the employment outlook for the career: whether the total number of people employed in this career will increase or decrease in the coming years and whether jobs in this field will be easy or hard to find. These predictions are based on economic conditions, the size and makeup of the population, foreign competition, and new technology. Terms such as "faster than the average," "about as fast as the average," and "slower than the average," are terms used by the U.S. Department of Labor to describe job growth predicted by government data.

Keep in mind that these predictions are general statements. No one knows for sure what the future will be like. Also remember that the employment outlook is a general statement about an industry and does not necessarily apply to everyone. A determined and talented person may be able to find a job in an industry or career with the worst kind of outlook. And a person without ambition and the proper training will find it difficult to find a job in even a booming industry or career field.

Where can I find more information?

Each chapter includes a sidebar called "For More Info." It lists organizations that you can contact to find out more about the field and careers in the field. You will find names, addresses, phone numbers, and Web sites.

Extras

Every chapter has a few extras. There are photos that show government workers in action. There are sidebars and notes on ways to explore the field, related jobs, fun facts, profiles of people in the field, or lists of Web sites and books that might be helpful. At the end of the book you will find a glossary and an index. The glossary gives brief definitions of words that relate to education, career training, or employment that you may be unfamiliar with. The index includes all the job titles mentioned in the book. It is followed by a list of general government-related Web sites.

It's not too soon to think about your future. We hope you discover several possible career choices. Happy hunting!

Ambassadors

What Ambassadors Do

About 180 countries in the world host U.S. embassies in their capital cities. An embassy is the headquarters of a U.S. diplomatic mission. As head of the mission, the *ambassador* represents the president and the general interests of the United States. Ambassadors handle issues such as security, trade, tourism, environmental protection, and health care. They help establish international agreements such as nuclear test bans and ozone layer protection. They promote peace and stability and open new markets.

Ambassadors meet with government officials and private citizens of the host country. They identify subjects that are of concern to both the United States and the host country, such as medical research, the development of new technologies, or human rights. When the host country suffers natural disasters, epidemics, and other problems, ambassadors might ask for financial and personnel aid from the United States.

Ambassadors usually are based in the U.S. embassy in a country's capital city. They also travel across the country to learn about its cities, towns, and rural areas. They try to promote a good, positive attitude toward the United States. When important U.S. visitors—such as the president, the first lady, and the secretary of state—arrive in the country, ambassadors serve as hosts, introducing them to the country and its officials.

Ambassadors are nominated for their positions by the president, and the nomination must then be confirmed by the Senate. They hold the post for only a few years.

Education and Training

Many ambassadors work up through the ranks of the Foreign Service or gain recognition in other areas, such as academics and business. For any work that involves international relations, you need a well-rounded education. English, history, math, social studies, and foreign language classes are important. Look for opportunities to travel to other countries with student groups. Ambassadors have

EXPLORING

• Join a foreign language club at your school.

• Student exchange programs offer opportunities to spend time in another country.

•The People to People Student Ambassador Program offers summer travel opportunities to students in grades six through 12. To learn about the expenses, destinations, and application process, visit this Web site: http://www. studentambassadors. org.

• Visit the Department of State Web site at http://www.state.gov to read the biographies of ambassadors around the world. The site also has links to individual embassy Web sites.

EARLY AMBASSADORS

Early in U.S. history, diplomacy was recognized as important to a strong government. Benjamin Franklin, John Adams, John Jay, and Francis Dana were chosen for their intelligence, strength of character, and powers of persuasion to enlist the support of foreign countries for American independence. Benjamin Franklin was so successful in his commission to France, the French put his picture on watches, jewelry, and even snuffboxes. And the women of France had their hair done to resemble the fur caps Franklin wore. However, not all diplomats enjoyed such stardom; Francis Dana spent a cold, unproductive two years in Russia, unable to speak the language, and incapable of convincing Catherine II to support American independence.

The State Department was established in 1789 and placed under the direction of Thomas Jefferson, the first U.S. secretary of state and the senior member of President Washington's cabinet. It was his responsibility to initiate foreign policy on behalf of the U.S. government, advise the president on matters related to foreign policy, and administer the foreign affairs of the United States.

Before the invention of radio, telegraph, and telephone, ambassadors were entrusted to make final, binding decisions on behalf of the United States. Today's ambassadors represent the president and actively contribute to international relations, but they are more restricted in their powers.

college degrees and many have master's degrees and doctorates in fields such as international relations, economics, political science, and mathematics.

All Foreign Service officers are required to pass written and oral examinations. These examinations test your understanding of government institutions, geography, the history of the United States, foreign policy, and other subjects. An officer must work for many years, with a great deal of success, to be promoted to Career Ambassador, the highest rank of Foreign Service officer.

Earnings

Starting salaries for new Foreign Service officers without a bachelor's degree are $29,911 a year. With a bachelor's or advanced degree and knowledge of a foreign language, officers can earn from $33,665 to $39,952 to start. Junior officers make up to $49,136 a year. Career officers make between $50,960 and $100,897, while senior Foreign Service officers earn $106,200 to $118,400.

Outlook

Since the end of the Cold War, diplomatic relations have changed. In the last decade, the U.S. international affairs budget has been drastically cut. Foreign aid funding has dropped from $20 billion in 1985, to $12.8 billion in 1999. Part of an ambassador's job is analyzing budgets to determine where cutbacks can be made. Experts worry that further cuts will not only hurt international trade but will result in disharmony among nations.

FOR MORE INFO

For more information about careers with the Foreign Service, the exam, and internships, visit the State Department's Web site, or contact:
Foreign Service
U.S. Department of State
PO Box 9317
Rosslyn Station
Arlington, VA 22219
703-875-7490
http://www.state.gov

For information about careers in U.S. embassies, contact:
American Foreign Service Association
2101 E Street, NW
Washington, DC 20037
800-704-AFSA
http://www.afsa.org

Council of American Ambassadors
888 17th Street, Suite 901
Washington, DC 20006
202-296-3757
http://www.his.com~council

Despite these budget cuts, the number of responsibilities of ambassadors and Foreign Service officers has increased. Drug trade, nuclear smuggling, and terrorism are some of the issues confronting embassies today.

City Managers

A Bit of History

The "council-manager" form of government is truly American in origin. Before the government reforms of the early 1900s, cities were run by city councils or boards of aldermen. Because of rigged elections and other corruption by aldermen, a mayoral form of government was begun. The council-manager form of government also had its beginnings around this time. Some southern towns began to develop council-manager forms of government as early as 1908.

Dayton, Ohio, became the first large city to put the council-manager form into place in 1913 with Colonel Henry M. Waite as the first city manager. According to the International City/County Management Association, more than 3,056 cities and 144 counties operate in the council-manager form today. More than 71 million people live in these communities.

What City Managers Do

City managers direct the day-to-day operations of a city. They determine what the city needs, such as the improvement of air quality, better public transportation, or new parks. They make long-range plans for the city as it grows larger.

One important job of a city manager is to prepare a yearly budget for the city. The budget outlines the amount of money the city plans to spend on law enforcement, public health, recreation, economic development, and other services, such as garbage pickup and street improvements. City managers stay aware of the needs and interests of the members of the community, and keep everyone informed of city projects and proposals.

City managers work in cities that have a council-manager form of government. In this system, all power is held by an elected council. A principal elected official, usually the *mayor,* coordinates and leads

Mathew Hohmann

City managers work closely with mayors and other local officials in planning their cities' futures.

EXPLORING

• **Become involved in student government or serve as an officer for a school club to get experience in how groups are organized and run.**

• **Work for the school newspaper to learn about budgets, issues at your school, and school administration.**

• **Pay attention to your local government, including the activities of the mayor, city or county council members, and other officials.**

• **Visit your city's Web site to learn more about its government, history, and special issues.**

the council. He or she makes the decisions on policies and programs, approves them, and meets with the public and news media to discuss the issues. City managers are appointed by the city council. They work behind the scenes to put these programs in place. They oversee the daily operations of a community according to the policies adopted by the council.

City managers may appoint department heads and a staff to coordinate the various activities of the government. These people have supervisory duties over tax collection, public health, public buildings, law enforcement, and all the other details of keeping a city or town working smoothly. Department heads prepare reports for their city managers, who distribute them to the city council.

Education and Training

Government and social studies classes will teach you about how cities and counties are organized. Math skills are important for working on budgets and statistics, and preparing financial reports.

To work as a city manager, you must have a bachelor's degree. A master's degree in public administration will open even more job opportunities. Some city managers have a master's or other advanced degree in political science, urban planning, or law. To be eligible for city management jobs, you usually must pass a civil service examination. New college graduates may begin as assistants in a

CITY MANAGERS ARE GOOD FOR CITIES

Reason Public Policy Institute conducted a study of America's 44 largest cities, called Competitive Cities Report Card. It shows that "cities run by city managers are 50 percent more likely to be efficient in the delivery of public services than are cities run by elected mayors," says an article in *American City and County* magazine. Of the top 10 most efficient cities, five operate under the council-manager form of government. The top 10 list includes:

Phoenix, Arizona
El Paso, Texas
Tulsa, Oklahoma
Memphis, Tennessee
Nashville, Tennessee
San Diego, California
Dallas, Texas
Virginia Beach, Virginia
Indianapolis, Indiana
San Antonio, Texas

city manager's office. There you learn to solve various city management problems. After several years of experience, you may become qualified to be a city manager.

Earnings

City managers' earnings vary according to the size of the city, its geographical location, and the manager's education and experience. A survey by the International City/County Management Association says that salaries ranged from $30,000 to $180,000 in 1999. Salaries at the low end are generally for managers of cities with populations below 2,500. The higher salaries are earned by managers of cities with populations over 1 million. The average of the mean salaries from across the country was about $73,650.

Outlook

Although city management is a growing profession, the field is still small. Applicants with only a bachelor's degree will have the most difficulty finding employment. Even an entry-level job often requires an advanced degree. The issues that affect a city are constantly changing. Future city managers will need to focus on clean air

FOR MORE INFO

For more information about the county-manager form of government, and the issues effecting today's cities, contact:

International City/County Management Association.
777 North Capitol Street, NE, Suite 500
Washington, DC 20002-4201
202-289-4262
http://www.icma.org

National League of Cities
1301 Pennsylvania Avenue, NW
Washington, DC 20004
202-626-3000
http://www.nlc.org

regulations, promoting diversity, providing affordable housing, new policing methods, and revitalizing old downtown areas.

RELATED JOBS

Campaign Workers
Congressional Aides
Lobbyists
Political Scientists
Press Secretaries
Regional and Local Officials
Urban and Regional Planners
State and Federal Officials

Congressional Aides

Do Congress Members Need Aides?

Ever since members of Congress first began to hire secretaries to assist with office duties, the role of congressional aides has stirred controversy. In the early 1800s, congressmen worried they would look incapable of handling the responsibilities of their jobs if they relied too much on assistants. This concern still exists today. Some members of Congress say that having too many aides distances the senators and representatives from voters, and legislation.

Even critics, however, admit that aides are very important. The Legislative Reorganization Act of 1946 allows each House and Senate standing committee to employ a campaign staff of four professional and six clerical workers. Another Reorganization Act, passed in 1970, increased the number of professional staff to six members.

What Congressional Aides Do

Congressional aides help *senators* and *representatives* do their jobs. Senators and representatives appoint aides to serve on their staffs as assistants, press secretaries, office managers, legislative correspondents, and state or district directors.

Congressional aides play important roles in helping senators and representatives get elected and reelected. They organize fund-raising campaigns and distribute information about the Congress member's qualifications and opinions. Since the main responsibility of Congress is to make federal laws, members of Congress spend six months of each year in Washington, D.C., where they meet from January until the end of July. This means that they have two offices: one in the nation's capital and the other in their home state. Their aides help business run smoothly in both offices.

Jay Barnard

Congressional aides need good communication skills. They must listen carefully to their employers and also be able to express their own ideas.

Aides work on either a personal or committee staff. A committee staff focuses primarily on creating and passing legislation. The personal staff deals with matters concerning the home district or state. Some of the duties of aides include sorting mail, keeping files in order, word processing, answering the telephone, maintaining a computer base of constituents (voters from the home state), conducting opinion polls, doing research for pending bills, and receiving drop-in visitors. They often serve as a sounding board for their Congress member's ideas. Some aides may write speeches and position papers that describe how a senator or representative feels about a certain issue.

EXPLORING

• Volunteer to work on campaigns for local elections.

• Keep up with current events by reading newspapers and news magazines. With an understanding of current issues, you can take a stand and express your opinions to your local, state, and federal representatives.

Education and Training

Courses in U.S. government, civics, social studies, and history will provide a good foundation for any career in government. Congressional aides have bachelor's degrees, usually in political science, journalism, or economics. Most committee aides have advanced degrees in law or journalism. They attend committees with the Congress member and meet with lobbyists and special interest groups.

You need good writing and speaking skills to work as an aide. You must be courteous and efficient. You need to be able to analyze information and do research. You must also be able to organize the enormous amount of paperwork and information that comes into a Congress member's office.

CONGRESS BY THE NUMBERS

Each state sends two senators to Congress. The number of House representatives from each state depends on the state's population. After the census of 2000, membership in the House of Representatives is:

State	#	State	#	State	#	State	#
Alabama	7	Indiana	9	Nebraska	3	Pennsylvania	19
Alaska	1	Iowa	5	Nevada	3	Rhode Island	2
Arizona	8	Kansas	4	New Hampshire	2	South Carolina	6
Arkansas	4	Kentucky	6	New Jersey	13	South Dakota	1
California	53	Louisiana	7	New Mexico	3	Tennessee	9
Colorado	7	Maine	2	New York	29	Texas	32
Connecticut	5	Maryland	8	North Carolina	13	Utah	3
Delaware	1	Massachusetts	10	North Dakota	1	Vermont	1
Florida	25	Michigan	15	Ohio	18	Virginia	11
Georgia	13	Minnesota	8	Oklahoma	5	Washington	9
Hawaii	2	Mississippi	4	Oregon	3	West Virginia	3
Idaho	2	Missouri	9			Wisconsin	9
Illinois	19	Montana	1			Wyoming	1

Total senators 100
Total representatives 435

Earnings

Congressional aide salaries for most positions are higher in the Senate than they are in the House. According to the Congressional Management Foundation, an administrative assistant (chief of staff) earns an average of $116,500 a year working for a senator, and about $97,600 a year working for a representative. Legislative directors earn $91,438 in the Senate, and $61,000 in the House. Legislative assistants make about $48,300 in the Senate, and $33,196 in the House. Aides who perform clerical duties—such as computer operators, correspondents, and receptionists—earn around $23,000.

Outlook

Members of Congress will continue to regularly hire aides. The number of aides hired will be affected by budget concerns and public opinion that Congress members rely too much on their staffs. An aide's job duties can be affected by voter

FOR MORE INFO

For information about individual Congress members and legislation, contact:.
Office of Senator (Name)
U.S. Senate
Washington, DC 20510
202-224-3121
http://www.senate.gov

Office of Congressperson (Name)
U.S. House of Representatives
Washington, DC 20510
202-224-3121
http://www.house.gov

To learn about job openings in Senate offices, contact:
Senate Placement Office
Room SH-142B
Washington, DC 20510
202-228-5627

concerns, the political party in power, and current issues.

In the future, aides will be working with a constituency much more knowledgeable about legislation because of the Internet. The Internet will also help aides in their research of bills and their gauging of public views.

Corrections Officers

What Corrections Officers Do

Corrections officers guard people who have been arrested and are awaiting trial. They also guard those who have been tried, found guilty, and sentenced to prison time. They search prisoners and their cells for weapons and drugs. They check locks, bars on windows and doors, and gates for signs of tampering.

Prisoners must be under guard at all times—while eating, sleeping, exercising, and working. Corrections officers count prisoners from time to time to make sure they are all present. Some officers are stationed at gates and on towers to prevent escapes. Corrections officers carefully observe the attitude and behavior of prison inmates and watch for potential conflicts. The officers try to settle disputes before they erupt into violence. When a disturbance or crime occurs at the prison, officers are responsible for stopping it and helping to find the cause.

Corrections officers give work assignments to prisoners and supervise them as they work. They check prisoners' cells for unclean conditions and fire hazards. Sometimes they may check prisoners' mail for forbidden items. If a prisoner is injured, they give first aid. When visitors come to the prison, officers check their identification before taking them to the visiting area.

In small towns, corrections officers may act as deputy sheriffs or police officers when they are not performing guard duties. Many corrections officers work at prisons, prison camps, and reform schools run by state governments. Others work at city and county jails. Still others work at prisons run by the federal government. Many correctional facilities are run by private companies.

Education and Training

Corrections officers generally must be at least 18 to 21 years old and have a high school diploma. Many positions require some postsecondary education or related work experience. Most states and some local governments train corrections officers on the job. They spend two to six months under the supervision of experienced officers. The federal government

EXPLORING

• Look for books in your library on crime, prisons, and law enforcement. Here are some suggestions:

Alcatraz Prison in American History by Marilyn Tower Oliver (Enslow Publishers, 1998).

Crime and Punishment: Changing Attitudes 1900-2000 by Alison Brownlie (Raintree/Steck Vaughn, 1999).

Go to Jail: A Look at Prisons through the Ages by Peter Kent (Millbrook Press, 1998).

Outlaws, Mobsters & Crooks: From the Old West to the Internet by Jane Hoehner and Marie Macnee, eds. (U^Xx^XL, 1998).

and some states have special schools for training corrections officers in programs that last from four to eight weeks.

In many states, you must pass physical fitness, eyesight, and hearing tests. Some states require one or two years of experience in corrections or related police work.

Earnings

According to a 1999 national survey in *Correction Compendium,* salaries range widely from one state to another. In California, for example, corrections officers start at $14,600, while New Jersey corrections officers earn $34,100. Beginning corrections officers at the federal level earn $20,600 to $23,000 depending on the location. Sergeants and other supervisors start at $41,000. The average for all federal corrections officers and sergeants is $36,500 a year.

The U.S. Department of Labor reports that median annual earnings of corrections officers were $28,540 in 1998. Salaries ranged from $18,000 to $46,300.

Outlook

Most jobs will be found in relatively large institutions located near cities. The increasing use of private companies and privately run prisons may limit somewhat the growth of jobs in this field as these companies are more likely to keep a close eye on the bottom line. Use of new technologies, such as surveillance equipment, automatic gates, and other devices, may also allow institutions to employ fewer officers.

Employment in this field is expected to increase much faster than the average for all jobs, according to the U.S. Department of Labor. The war on illegal drugs, new tough-on-crime laws, and increasing

FOR MORE INFO

Federal Bureau of Prisons
National Recruitment Office
320 First Street, NW, Room 460
Washington, DC 20534
cmahan@bop.gov
http://www.bop.gov

American Correctional Association
4380 Forbes Boulevard
Lanham, MD 20706
800-222-5646
http://www.corrections.com/aca

American Probation and Parole Association
2760 Research Park Drive
Lexington, KY 40511-8410
859-244-8203
http://www.appa-net.org

The Corrections Connection Network
159 Burgin Parkway
Quincy, MA 02169
617-471-4445
http://www.corrections.com

mandatory sentencing policies will create a need for more prisons and more corrections officers.

Customs Officials

What Customs Officials Do

Customs officials make sure illegal merchandise (called contraband), such as drugs, is not smuggled into the United States. They are employed by the federal government to enforce the laws that regulate goods coming into the country (imports) and goods leaving the country (exports). Customs officials work at airports, seaports, and border crossings in every entry and exit point of the United States.

Customs officials need to be observant and crafty to search out all the possible hiding places in luggage or clothes where people might hide contraband. Federal law prevents other items besides drugs from being transported across borders, including certain plants and foods that could carry insects and disease. Importing many species of animals, and products made from them, is also prohibited by law.

Customs officials check the contents of a traveler's suitcase.

At airports and seaports, customs officials check the luggage and personal items of airline and ship passengers and crew members as well as the ship's or airplane's cargo. They make sure that all merchandise is declared honestly, that duties are paid, and that no contraband is present. Customs officials also determine taxes, called duties, that people must pay on imports and exports. Travelers sometimes try to hide expensive imports to avoid paying high duties on them. Customs officials need to be as alert to these tax-evaders as to drug dealers. At border-crossing points, customs officials

EXPLORING

• The U.S. Customs Service has an Explorer program. It offers young adults the opportunity to experience law-enforcement activities related to Customs Service careers. To read more about this program, see http://www. customs.ustreas.gov/ career/career.htm.

check the baggage of travelers who come by car or train to and from Canada and Mexico.

The United States imports many products, which are then sold or used for industry, such as bales of cotton from India, rugs from Iran, diamonds from Africa, and wool from Ireland. Customs officials examine, count, weigh, gauge, measure, and sample commercial cargoes and check their figures against shipping papers. Then they figure how much import duty (tax) should be paid. *Customs warehouse officers* guard the goods on the pier or in the warehouse to prevent theft, damage, and fire.

Education and Training

If you are interested in working for the U.S. Customs Service, take courses in government, geography, social studies,

WHERE CUSTOMS OFFICIALS WORK

The customs territory of the United States is divided into nine regions that include the 50 states, the District of Columbia, Puerto Rico, and the U.S. Virgin Islands. In these regions there are about 300 ports of entry along land and sea borders. Customs inspectors may be assigned to any of these ports or to overseas work at airports, seaports, waterfronts, border stations, customs houses, or the U.S. Customs Service Headquarters in Washington, D.C.

A typical work schedule is eight hours a day, five days a week, but customs employees often work overtime or long into the night. United States entry and exit points must be supervised 24 hours a day, which means that workers rotate night shifts and weekend duty. Customs inspectors and patrol officers are sometimes assigned to one-person border points at remote locations, where they may perform immigration and agricultural inspections in addition to regular duties. They often risk physical injury from criminals violating customs regulations.

English, and history. If you wish to become a specialist in scientific or investigative aspects of the Customs Service, you need courses in the sciences, especially chemistry, and computer science will be helpful.

To be a customs worker, you must be a U.S. citizen, and at least 21 years old. You must have at least a high school diploma, but a college degree is preferred. If you do not have a college degree, you must have at least three years of related work experience. Customs inspectors, like all employees of the federal government, must pass a physical examination and undergo a security check. You must also pass a standardized test called the Professional and Administrative Career Examination.

Earnings

Entry-level customs officials earn between $22,000 and $27,000 a year. Most customs officials earn about $33,200. Supervisors earn from $40,200

FOR MORE INFO

U.S. Customs Service
Office of Human Resources
1300 Pennsylvania Avenue, NW
Washington, DC 20229
http://www.customs.ustreas.gov

to $48,200 to start. Federal employees in certain cities receive extra locality pay in addition to their salaries to allow for the higher cost of living in those areas.

Outlook

Employment for customs officials is steady and not affected by changes in the economy. There is more emphasis today on law enforcement, including the detection of illegally imported drugs and pornography and the prevention of exports of certain high-technology items. This means the prospects for steady employment are good.

Deputy U.S. Marshals

What Deputy U.S. Marshals Do

The U.S. Marshal Service is the oldest federal law enforcement agency. Since the time of George Washington, it has been responsible for upholding the law of the land. *Deputy U.S. marshals* are law enforcement officers who protect and enforce the decisions of the U.S. judiciary system, including judges, the Supreme Court, and the Department of Justice.

Deputy U.S. marshals transport federal criminals to prison, sometimes in government-owned jets. They are on guard in federal courtrooms to protect judges and jury members who are involved in important legal cases that put their lives in possible danger. They serve subpoenas, summonses, and other legal papers to people involved in federal court cases.

Marshals investigate and track down fugitives (criminals who are running from the law), even those who have escaped to another country. They also try to find fugitives in the United States who are wanted by foreign nations. In hunting down fugitives, marshals often work with state and local police departments and with other law enforcement agencies.

The Marshal Service operates the nation's witness relocation program. This program encourages witnesses to testify in federal trials even though it might put them in danger. The Marshal Service provides personal protection for witnesses until they testify in court. After the trial is over, the Marshal Service helps witnesses move to new locations and take on new names and identities to keep them safe.

U.S. marshals also operate the program for confiscating property that has been purchased with money gained from certain illegal activities such as drug dealing. The marshals seize houses, boats, and other property that criminals have purchased. They hold it and maintain it until the property is sold or put up for auction.

The Marshal Service can respond to emergency situations such as riots, terrorist incidents, or hostage situations when federal law is violated or federal property is endangered. A highly trained

EXPLORING

• If you are interested in more information about working as a deputy U.S. marshal, write directly to the Marshal Service. (See For More Info.)

• For more background, you can find an in-depth historical survey in *The Lawmen: United States Marshals and Their Deputies, 1789-1989* by Frederick S. Calhoun (Smithsonian Institution Press, 1990).

RELATED JOBS

Border Patrol Officers
Corrections Officers
Customs Officials
Detectives
FBI Agents
Intelligence Officers
Police Officers
Secret Service Special Agents

force of deputy U.S. marshals called the Special Operations Group (SOG) handles these situations. Deputies also protect shipments of weapons systems for the U.S. Air Force.

Education and Training

Deputy U.S. marshals are trained at the Federal Law Enforcement Training Center in Glynco Naval Air Station in Georgia. They complete a three-month training program that teaches them about laws, proper procedures, firearm use, and physical training.

To enter this program, you first take a civil service exam. You are then interviewed to see if you have the makings of a good deputy marshal. You must have at least some college education, work experience, or a combination of both. A point system weighs all the qualifications and determines who will be admitted. Competition for these jobs is strong—there is an average of 15 applicants for every opening.

THE FIRST MARSHALS

The Judiciary Act, passed by Congress in 1789, established not only the post of U.S. marshal but also the country's original federal court system. The act delegated two duties to the marshals: to enforce all precepts issued by the federal government and to protect and attend to the federal courts. Marshals were also authorized to hire one or more deputies.

The first 13 U.S. marshals, appointed by President George Washington, were confirmed by the U.S. Senate on September 26, 1789. Over the next year two more marshals were chosen. The 13 original states, as well as the districts of Kentucky and Maine, were each assigned a marshal. The number of marshals and deputies increased as the United States expanded westward, and with a rise in the country's population, some states were assigned more than one marshal. Today there are close to 2,500 deputy U.S. marshals assigned to more than 95 districts across the United States and Puerto Rico, Guam, the Virgin Islands, and the Northern Marianas.

Earnings

Beginning deputy U.S. marshals earn $20,588 annually. Those with bachelor's or advanced degrees in law enforcement, criminology, law, and other related disciplines are hired at $25,500 a year to start. Experienced deputy U.S. marshals earn about $37,700 a year, but deputy U.S. marshals certified in a specialty area may earn up to $45,200. Chief deputy marshals earn $55,000 a year and more. The top of the government pay scale for deputy U.S. marshals is $74,780 a year.

Outlook

There are close to 2,500 deputy U.S. marshals assigned to more than 95 districts across the United States and Puerto Rico, Guam, the Virgin Islands, and the Northern Marianas. Employment opportunities are expected to increase at an average rate through the next decade. Careers in law enforcement and security-related fields in general are expected to grow rapidly as federal and state governments pass new "tough-on-crime" legislation and the number of criminals continues to grow. Great increases in the crime rate will most likely prompt public pressures to increase hiring of law enforcement officials, including deputy U.S. marshals. Nonetheless, because of the prestige offered by this career and the generous benefits available to many careers in federal service, competition for available positions will remain strong.

FOR MORE INFO

To find out about this career, contact the marshal's office of your local federal district.
U.S. Marshal Service
Employment and Compensation Division
Field Staffing Branch
600 Army Navy Drive
Arlington, VA 22202-4210
202-307-9600
http://www.usdoj.gov/marshals

FBI Agents

The fingerprint section of the FBI Laboratory is the largest in the world. It has more than 250 million sets of fingerprints. The lab:
• Identifies and maintains fingerprint records for arrested criminal suspects, government employees, and people who apply for federal jobs.
• Posts notices about people wanted for crimes and for parole or probation violations.
• Examines physical evidence for fingerprints and provides court testimony on the results of exams.
• Trains agents in fingerprint science.
• Keeps fingerprint records of missing persons.
• Identifies amnesia victims and unknown deceased people.

What FBI Agents Do

The Federal Bureau of Investigation (FBI) is a government agency that trains *special agents* or *investigators* to report on people who are suspected of crimes against the United States. FBI agents also track down criminals who have broken federal laws. These crimes include bank robbery, kidnapping, theft, spying against the United States (espionage), and destroying U.S. property (sabotage). The FBI is responsible for investigating over 270 violations of federal law.

Agents send their reports and the evidence from their investigations to the criminal laboratory at the FBI headquarters in Washington, D.C. There they are filed in various departments such as fingerprinting, firearms, documents, or photography. This information is available to any law enforcement agency in the United States.

The work of FBI agents is top secret and often dangerous. Agents cannot talk

An FBI agent searches through old files and new faxes to collect information on crime suspects.

Mathew Hohmann

about their assignments with family or friends. They often work alone, but they keep in touch with law enforcement agencies all over the world. Their travels take them to a variety of cities where they may investigate people and take part in arrests and raids.

Unlike police officers, agents wear ordinary clothes so they will not bring attention to themselves. They usually carry some form of identification so that others will know they are acting on behalf of the U.S. government. Those who do dangerous work carry guns for protection.

EXPLORING

• Ask your librarian to help you find books and other resources on the FBI and crime fighting. Here are some suggestions:

The Federal Bureau of Investigation by Dynise Balcavage (Chelsea House Publishers, 2000).

Crime Detection by Chris Oxlade (Heineman Library, 1997).

Crime Science by Vivien Bowers (Owl Communications, 1997).

Detective Dictionary: A Handbook for Aspiring Sleuths by Erich Ballinger (Lerner Publications Company, 1994).

• Visit the FBI Kids & Youth Educational Page at http://www.fbi.gov/kids/kids.htm.

Education and Training

To become an FBI agent, you must be a citizen of the United States and be 23 years old. You need at least one of the following: a degree from a law school; fluency in a foreign language; or a bachelor's degree in accounting, engineering, or computer science. If your degree is in another subject, you need three years of full-time work experience after college or a graduate degree and two years of work experience.

Applicants must also pass a series of written and oral examinations. The exams test your knowledge of law and accounting, as well as your ability to investigate crimes. Before you are hired, your background is checked thoroughly and you must pass a physical fitness exam.

New agents complete an extensive 16-week training program at the FBI Academy at Quantico, Virginia. There you learn FBI rules and regulations, fingerprinting, firearm techniques, defensive tactics, and federal criminal law. After training, new agents are put on probation for a year. During this time you are supervised by a senior agent. If you

WORDS TO LEARN

The Bureau: The Federal Bureau of Investigation.

Method of operation (M.O.): The standard pattern someone uses to commit a crime.

Profile: A general description of a type of person who might commit a certain kind of crime. For example, the FBI creates profiles of serial killers and financial criminals.

Special agent: A government title for federal employees who investigate criminal violations.

Street agent: An FBI agent not in management who conducts investigations.

Surveillance: To gather information by following, observing, or listening to people.

Wire tap: Electronic surveillance over the telephone.

are found to be fit after a year, you are hired permanently.

Earnings

Special agent trainees at the Quantico training facility are paid about $36,600. Graduates assigned to field offices earn about $42,000 a year. Experienced special agents average $57,300 a year and the most experienced agents earn about $67,800 a year. Supervisory positions begin at $79,700. Some agents then move into a different employment category called the Senior Executive Service, where they earn more than $100,000 a year.

Outlook

In 1999, the FBI employed approximately 11,400 special agents. Job vacancies open up as agents retire, advance, or resign, but turnover is low because most agents stay with the FBI throughout their working lives.

The FBI has increased the number of agents in recent years

FOR MORE INFO

For information about a career as an FBI agent, contact a local field office or write to the following address:
The Federal Bureau of Investigation
J. Edgar Hoover Building
935 Pennsylvania Avenue, NW
Washington, DC 20535-0001
202-324-3000
http://www.fbi.gov

because of the growing number of organized crimes and white-collar crimes. But growth in the numbers of new agents is limited, so competition for openings is extremely strong.

RELATED JOBS

Crime Analysts
Cryptographic Technicians
Deputy U.S. Marshals
Detectives
Forensic Experts
Intelligence Officers
Police Officers
Polygraph Examiners
Secret Service Special Agents

Fish and Game Wardens

Meet Judie Miller, Refuge Ranger

Judie Miller is a refuge ranger and public affairs officer at the Minnesota Valley National Wildlife Refuge in Bloomington, Minnesota. She is responsible for outreach at the refuge, "which means that I need to inform not only the public, but our internal audiences about our mission and what we are doing."

Miller notes that "refuge ranger" is a general title that includes law enforcement workers, environmental educators, public affairs officers and volunteers. "My job also includes handling a number of special events at Minnesota Valley," says Miller. "For example, I coordinate the National Wildlife Refuge Week events at this refuge. I do many other outreach jobs, such as creating and writing newsletters and press releases, to get word out to people about our refuge."

What Fish and Game Wardens Do

Fish and game wardens are also called *wildlife conservationists, wildlife inspectors, refuge rangers,* and *refuge officers.* They protect wildlife, manage resources, and also perform public information and law enforcement tasks.

The conservation of fish and wildlife is a responsibility that grows more complex each year, especially with growing pollution and environmental changes. To accomplish its mission, the U.S. Fish and Wildlife Service, for example, employs many of the country's best biologists, wildlife managers, engineers, realty specialists, law enforcement agents, and others who work to save endangered and threatened species; conserve migratory birds and inland fisheries; provide expert advice to other federal agencies, industry, and foreign governments; and manage more than 700 offices and field stations. These personnel are working in every state and territory from the Arctic Ocean to the South Pacific, and from the Atlantic to the Caribbean.

Wildlife inspectors and special agents are two jobs that fall in the fish and game warden category of the U.S. Fish and Wildlife Service. Wildlife inspectors monitor the legal trade of federally protected fish and wildlife and intercept illegal imports and exports. At points of entry into the United States, wildlife inspectors examine shipping containers, live animals, wildlife products such as animal skins, and documents. Inspectors, who work closely with special agents, may seize shipments as evidence, conduct investigations, and testify in courts of law.

Special agents of the U.S. Fish and Wildlife Service are trained criminal investigators who enforce federal wildlife laws throughout the country. Special agents conduct investigations, which may include surveillance, undercover work, making arrests, and preparing cases for court. These agents enforce migratory bird regulations and investigate illegal trade in protected wildlife.

Refuge rangers or refuge managers work at the more than 550 national refuges

EXPLORING

• Visit your local nature centers and park preserves often. Attend any classes or special lectures they offer. There may be opportunities to volunteer to help clean up sites, plant trees, or maintain pathways and trails.
• Get to know your local wildlife. What kind of insects, birds, fish, and other animals live in your area?
• Here are some reading suggestions:
And Then There Was One: The Mysteries of Extinction by Margery Facklam (Little Brown & Co., 1993).
The National Wildlife Federation's Wildlife Watcher's Handbook: A Guide to Observing Animals in the Wild by Joe La Tourrette (Owlet, 1997).
The Wildlife Detectives: How Forensic Scientists Fight Crimes Against Nature by Donna M. Jackson, Wendy Shattil, and Robert Rozinski (Houghton Miflin Co., 2000).

GOVERNMENTS STEP IN TO CURB EXTINCTION

For centuries, wildlife has suffered because of the actions of human beings. Bows, rifles, and shotguns made it easier for people to kill game. ("Game" is any fish, birds, or mammals that are hunted non-commercially for food, sport, or both.) Some species of animals have been hunted to extinction. Forests have been cleared, swamps drained, and rivers dammed to clear the way for agriculture and industry. These activities have harmed or destroyed large areas of plant and wildlife habitat.

Beginning in the late 19th century, there was growing concern for vanishing wildlife. The governments of the United States and other nations started conservation programs and passed laws to protect wildlife and set aside national parks and other reserves.

The main agency assigned to the conservation of animals and their habitats in this country is the U.S. Fish and Wildlife Service, created in 1856. It is responsible for the scientific development of commercial fisheries and the conservation of fish and wildlife.

across the country, protecting and conserving migratory and native species of birds, mammals, fish, endangered species, and other wildlife. Many of these refuges also offer outdoor recreational opportunities and educational programs.

Education and Training

Courses in biology and other sciences, geography, mathematics, social studies, and physical education will help you prepare for this career.

To become a fish and game warden you must have a bachelor's degree or three years of work experience. Higher positions require at least one year of graduate studies and some professional positions, such as biologist or manager, require master's or doctoral degrees.

On-the-job training is given for most positions. Special agents receive 18 weeks of formal training in criminal investigation and wildlife law enforcement techniques at the Federal Law Enforcement Training Center in Glynco, Georgia.

Earnings

In the wide variety of positions available at the U.S. Fish and Wildlife Service, salaries range from $18,000 up to $91,000 for more advanced positions. Law enforcement positions, especially special agents, receive higher salaries because their jobs are more dangerous.

Outlook

The largest number of jobs in the field are with the U.S. Fish and Wildlife Service and other agencies of the Department of the Interior, such as the National Park Service. State agencies, such as Departments of Natural Resources or Departments of Parks and Recreation, also have positions in this area.

FOR MORE INFO

You can learn more about fish and game wardens and related employment opportunities through the following organizations:

U.S. Fish and Wildlife Service
Department of the Interior
1849 C Street, NW
Washington, DC 20240
703-358-2120
http://www.fws.gov

U.S. National Park Service
Department of the Interior
1849 C Street, NW
Washington, DC 20240
202-208-6843
http://www.nps.gov

Employment growth in this field depends on politics and government. Some administrations spend more on wildlife concerns, while others make cutbacks in this area.

RELATED JOBS

Biologists
Ecologists
Naturalists
Park Rangers
Range Managers

Foreign Service Workers

What Foreign Service Officers Do

As members of the State Department, *foreign service officers* represent the United States throughout all parts of the world. They meet with government officials from other countries and report to the State Department on issues that could affect the United States. Officers also issue passports and give visas to persons visiting or moving to the United States. They help protect U.S. citizens in foreign countries, and help encourage U.S. trade overseas.

Specific job duties depend on an officer's area of expertise and the requirements of the overseas office. *Administrative officers,* for example, work in embassies and manage the day-to-day operations of the office. They plan budgets and hire local workers. They purchase and look after government property, sign contracts for office space and housing, and make arrangements for shipping and travel.

Consular officers provide medical, legal, and travel assistance to U.S. citizens traveling abroad in cases of accidents or emergencies. For example, they help those without money return home, help find lost relatives, and advise American prisoners in foreign jails. They also issue visas to foreign nationals who want to enter the United States.

Political officers pay attention to local developments and reactions to U.S. policy. They stay in close contact with foreign leaders and watch for changes in attitudes and leadership that may affect the United States. They report their observations to Washington, D.C., and may suggest changes in U.S. policy.

Foreign service officers also try to help promote U.S. trade overseas. They advise U.S. firms about business practices in foreign countries where those firms might want to open a new business.

Education and Training

English, math, social studies, and foreign language classes are important for future foreign service officers. You need a strong desire for public service and an interest in other cultures. You must be able to communicate with people whose

EXPLORING

• Join a foreign language club at your school.

• Research student exchange programs if you're interested in spending several weeks in another country.

• The People to People Student Ambassador Program offers summer travel opportunities to students in grades six through 12. To learn about the expenses, destinations, and application process, visit its Web site at http://www.student ambassadors.org.

RELATED JOBS

Ambassadors
Congressional Aides
Federal and State Officials
Lobbyists
Political Scientists
Press Secretaries
Regional and Local Officials

PROFILE: JAMES PROSSER

James Prosser spent 36 years with the Foreign Service. He is now retired and visits academic and civic organizations to lecture about the history of the Foreign Service.

James's interest in foreign cultures started when he was very young. "Back in the 1930s," he says, "I built a crystal radio set which enabled me to listen to distant radio stations. That led me to discover shortwave listening, and soon I was listening to foreign countries."

As an officer, James worked in the telecommunications and computer fields as an operator, engineer, manager, and international negotiator. He speaks German, French, and Italian. His experiences included running a communications center and shortwave radio station in the Belgian Congo (now the Democratic Republic of the Congo) during the country's postcolonial independence. In 1967, France expelled North Atlantic Treaty Organization headquarters and James was placed in charge of moving the U.S. communications elements of NATO to Belgium, as well as designing the new communications facilities there. James also worked with Russians on the SALT (Strategic Arms Limitation Talks) delegations. James has served in Germany, Italy, Kenya, and other countries.

language, customs, and culture are different from your own.

Almost all officers have college degrees and many have master's degrees or doctorates in fields such as economics, political science, and mathematics. All foreign service officers are required to pass written and oral examinations. These examinations test applicants on their understanding of government institutions, geography, the history of the United States, foreign policy, and other subjects.

According to the American Foreign Service Association, foreign service officers need knowledge of proper English usage; U.S. society, culture, history, government, political systems, and the Constitution; world geography; and world political and social issues. In addition, all foreign service officers should know basic accounting, statistics and mathematics, and basic economic principles and trends.

Earnings

Earnings vary depending on experience, education, and foreign language skills. Starting salaries for new officers without a bachelor's degree are $29,911 a year. With a bachelor's or advanced degree and knowledge of a foreign language, officers can earn from $33,665 to $39,952 to start. Junior officers make up to $49,136 a year. Career officers make between $50,960 and $100,897, while senior foreign service officers earn $106,200 to $118,400.

Outlook

There are currently about 4,000 people working for the Foreign Service in Washington, D.C., and overseas. The number of positions varies every year, and may be affected in the future by funding cutbacks in diplomacy and international affairs.

FOR MORE INFO

The U.S. Department of State has career information on its Web site, along with information about internships, the history of the Foreign Service, and current officers and embassies. Or write to request brochures.
Foreign Service
U.S. Department of State
2201 C Street, NW
Washington, DC 20520
202-647-4000
http://www.state.gov

For information about Foreign Service careers, contact:
American Foreign Service Association
2101 E Street, NW
Washington, DC 20037
800-704-AFSA
http://www.afsa.org

According to the American Foreign Service Association, foreign service officers of the future will need management skills and knowledge of issues, such as science and technology, including the global fight against AIDS, efforts to save the environment, anti-narcotics efforts, and trade.

Health and Regulatory Inspectors

Where Inspectors Work

Approximately 163,000 people work as health and regulatory inspectors. State governments employ about 34 percent. The federal government employs 31 percent, mainly in the Departments of Agriculture, Defense, Justice, Labor, and Treasury. Local governments employ 18 percent. The U.S. Postal Service and private industry (mainly insurance companies, hospitals, education, and manufacturing firms) employ the remaining 17 percent.

What Health and Regulatory Inspectors Do

In the United States, the government passes laws to protect the health and safety of the public. *Health and regulatory inspectors* enforce those laws. Some health and regulatory inspectors work for the federal government. Others work for state and local governments. These inspectors have different titles depending on the type of work they do. There are many different types of inspectors.

Food and drug inspectors check companies that produce, store, handle, and market food, drugs, and cosmetics. They use scales, thermometers, chemical testing kits, ultraviolet lights, and cameras. They look for evidence to determine whether a product is harmful to the public's health or does not meet other standards for safety.

Agricultural inspectors make sure that we receive reliable and safe fruits, vegetables, grains, and dairy products. They

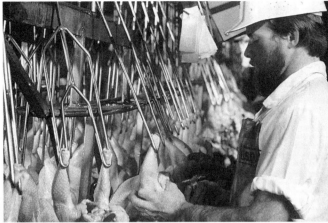

A health inspector examines chickens in a processing plant.

check not only domestic products but also products shipped to the United States from foreign countries. Some of these inspectors check aircraft, ships, and railway cars to make sure that no illegal products enter the United States.

Environmental health inspectors enforce standards of cleanliness in food processing plants, restaurants, hospitals, and other industries. They make sure that food is safe, garbage is disposed of properly, and water and air quality meet government standards.

Customs inspectors enforce the laws that regulate imports and exports. They inspect cargo coming into and leaving the United States. They determine if the cargo is legal and how much tax, if any, must be paid on it. Customs inspectors also check the baggage of people enter-

EXPLORING

• To learn more about health and regulatory inspection, visit these Web sites:

Agency for Toxic Substances and Disease Registry, Office of Children's Health Facts About Toxic Substances and the Environment
http://www.atsdr.cdc.gov/child/students.html

Consumer Product Safety Commission
http://www.cpsc.gov/kids/kids.html

EPA Superfund
http://www.epa.gov/superfund

FDA Kids
http://www.fda.gov/oc/opacom/kids/default.htm

USEPA Explorer's Club
http://www.epa.gov/kids

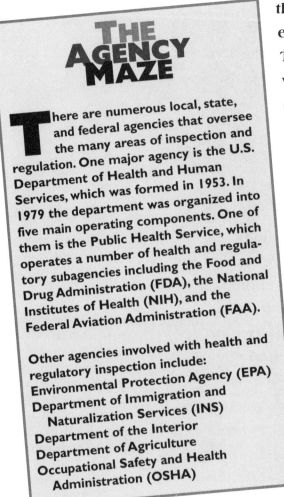

THE AGENCY MAZE

There are numerous local, state, and federal agencies that oversee the many areas of inspection and regulation. One major agency is the U.S. Department of Health and Human Services, which was formed in 1953. In 1979 the department was organized into five main operating components. One of them is the Public Health Service, which operates a number of health and regulatory subagencies including the Food and Drug Administration (FDA), the National Institutes of Health (NIH), and the Federal Aviation Administration (FAA).

Other agencies involved with health and regulatory inspection include:
Environmental Protection Agency (EPA)
Department of Immigration and
    Naturalization Services (INS)
Department of the Interior
Department of Agriculture
Occupational Safety and Health
    Administration (OSHA)

the safety and health of employees in the workplace. They inspect machinery, working conditions, and equipment to make sure that proper safety precautions are used. They monitor noise and air pollution, chemical exposure, and hazardous waste.

Education and Training

If you want to become a health and regulatory inspector, you must earn a bachelor's degree. Courses that are good preparation include biology, health, chemistry, agriculture, earth sciences, and shop.

ing and leaving the country to make sure that all required taxes have been paid and that nothing is being smuggled (carried illegally) in the baggage.

Occupational safety and health inspectors are responsible for

Health and regulatory inspectors are highly trained professionals who must have excellent knowledge of federal, state, and local laws. In addition, some inspectors have to pass written examinations relating to the type of inspections they will perform. Federal inspectors must pass the Professional and Administrative Career Examination. Inspectors also usually receive on-the-job training.

Earnings

Most federally employed health and regulatory inspectors receive starting salaries around $25,500 to $31,200. The median annual salary for all inspectors is $36,800. Some earn more than $72,280 a year.

Salaries vary depending on the job title. For example, occupational safety and health inspectors earn about $54,000, inspectors for consumer safety earn $37,300, customs inspectors earn $40,020, environmental protection specialists earn $58,000, and quality assurance inspectors earn $50,600 a year. Health and regulatory inspectors for state and local governments generally earn salaries lower than those paid by the federal government.

FOR MORE INFO

Occupational Safety and Health Administration
U.S. Department of Labor
Public Affairs Office, Room 3647
200 Constitution Avenue, NW
Washington, DC 20210
202-693-1999
http://www.osha.gov

Public Health Service
Department of Health
and Human Services
200 Independence Avenue, SW
Washington, DC 20201
202-619-0257
http://phs.os.dhhs.gov/phs

Environmental Protection Agency
401 M Street, SW
Washington, DC 20460
202-260-2090
http://www.epa.gov

Outlook

The employment of health and regulatory inspectors is likely to grow about as fast as the average through 2008, according to the U.S. Department of Labor. There is growing public concern for the environment, safety, and quality products.

Lobbyists

What Lobbyists Do

Lobbyists try to persuade legislators and other public office holders to support the interests of their clients. Clients, for example, may have concerns about wildlife conservation, recycling, or the regulation of industries. Most trade associations, labor unions, and corporations rely on the skills of reliable, trustworthy lobbyists to speak for their interests in Washington, D.C.

To persuade legislators, lobbyists use pamphlets, studies, news releases, or other printed information. They give news conferences and plan lectures and other events to promote their issues. They meet individually with legislators. They also contact other individuals or groups who could benefit from the laws they hope to get passed. They encourage the public to contact their representatives and senators and ask them to support legislation. Sometimes, lobbyists form a coalition with other lobbyists to strengthen their position on a specific issue. Lobbyists also may contact regulatory agencies and testify at public hearings to enlist support for their clients' interests.

Some lobbyists are employed as "for-hire" lobbyists, who represent clients on a contractual basis. Others work as staff members of a company, industry, or organization. Most lobbyists who represent corporations (such as pharmaceutical companies and insurance companies) and public sector interests (such as trade associations and labor unions) are based in Washington, D.C. For-hire lobbyists may be based either in Washington, D.C., or in their home state.

Lobbyists must register with government authorities and submit reports on the money they collect and spend during lobbying activities.

Education and Training

If you are interested in a career as a lobbyist, classes in speech and communications are important. Political science and journalism classes are also helpful.

Lobbyists have undergraduate degrees in political science, journalism, or public relations. They often hold graduate

EXPLORING

• Get involved in school government. Serve on the student council or work on student election campaigns.

• Write for your school newspaper.

• Work on publicity and advertising for school and community organizations and events.

• Take part in fund-raising drives, especially the planning and coordination phases.

• Join the debate team or work for the school radio station to help you with communication and research skills.

degrees in law or political science, as well. Most lobbyists enter the career after earning a great deal of experience in another government career, such as with Congress as a legislative aide, or as a press secretary.

Earnings

A lobbyist's income depends on the size of the organization he or she represents. Experienced contract lobbyists with a solid client base can earn well over $100,000 a year and some make more than $500,000 a year. Beginning lobbyists may make less than $20,000 a year as they build a client base.

Many associations employ directors of government relations, who earn an average of

LOBBYISTS GAIN RESPECT

Lobbying has been a practice within government since colonial times. In the late 1700s, the term "lobbyist" was used to describe the special-interest representatives who gathered in the anteroom outside the legislative chamber in the New York state capitol. The term was sometimes a negative label. Political cartoonists frequently showed lobbyists as slick, cigar-chomping men attempting to buy favors. But in the 20th century, lobbyists came to be considered as experts in the fields that they represented. Members of Congress relied on them to provide information needed to evaluate legislation. During the New Deal in the 1930s, government spending in Washington greatly increased, and the number of lobbyists grew, too.

In 1946, the Federal Regulation of Lobbying Act was passed into law. The act requires that anyone who spends or receives money or anything of value in the interests of passing, modifying, or defeating legislation be registered and provide spending reports. Additional regulatory acts have been passed in the years since. Most recently, the Lobbying Disclosure Act of 1995 requires all lobbyists working at the federal level to be registered.

$90,424 a year, according to a 1998 study by the American Society of Association Executives.

Outlook

The number of special interest groups in the United States continues to grow, and they will need lobbyists to plead their causes before state and federal governments. However, lobbying doesn't directly earn a profit for a business, so the government relations department is often the first to suffer from budget cuts. The American League of Lobbyists believes that the career will remain stable.

The Internet and email will continue to develop as tools for lobbyists. Web pages can inform the public of policy issues and include ways to immediately send email messages to state and federal legislators. With this method, members of Congress can easily determine the feelings of their constituents based on the amount of email they receive.

FOR MORE INFO

For additional information about a career as a lobbyist, contact:
American League of Lobbyists
PO Box 30005
Alexandria, VA 22310
703-960-3011
http://www.alldc.org

For information about working with policy issues within a trade association, visit the ASAE Web site:
American Society of Association Executives
1575 I Street, NW
Washington DC 20005
202-626-2723
http://www.asaenet.org

RELATED JOBS

Campaign Workers
Congressional Aides
Federal and State Officials
Political Scientists
Press Secretaries
Regional and Local Officials

Military Workers

What Military Workers Do

The United States armed forces are made up of the Army, the Navy, the Coast Guard, the Air Force, and the Marines. The Army operates on land, the Navy at sea, the Coast Guard within U.S. waters, and the Air Force in the air. The Marine Corps is a part of the navy and participates in ship-to-shore operations.

The main purpose of the armed forces is to defend the nation in times of conflict. However, only about 15 percent of those who work in the military are trained for combat. The rest of the members of the armed forces perform other important work to keep the nation's defense operating smoothly.

Most members of the armed forces live and work at military bases located in the United States and other countries around the world. On military bases, there are jobs for clerks, cooks, mechanics, electronics experts, technicians, doctors, den-

A military career is full of challenges and rewards.

U.S. Armed Forces

tists, scientists, and computer specialists. The military branches employ their own police force and intelligence and communications experts. More unusual jobs also are available. For instance, the Marine Corps offers a special program for applicants with musical talent, to train participants to play in corps bands. In general, an enlistee, or someone just entering the military, is assigned a job based on his or her wishes and qualifications, as well as the needs of the service.

The armed forces require strict discipline from all personnel. Special military laws must be followed, and uniforms must be worn while on duty. Those who choose a

EXPLORING

Here are some books with more information on military careers:
Life in Army Basic Training by **Gene Gartman** (**Children's Press, 2000**).
Life in the Army Special Forces by **Robert C. Kennedy** (**Children's Press, 2000**).
U.S. Marine Corps Special Forces: Recon Marines by **G. F. Marte** and **Edward A. Voeller** (**Capstone Press, 2000**).
U.S. Air Force Special Forces: Combat Controllers by **Kim Covert** and **Robert V. Martens** (**Capstone Press, 2000**).
U.S. Navy Special Forces: Seal Team by **Michael Burgan** (**Capstone Press, 2000**).

career in the armed forces can expect to move many times and to be away from family, often for long periods of time. Life in the military is demanding, but it does have many rewards.

Education and Training

To apply for a position in the armed forces, you must be a U.S. citizen between 17 and 35 years of age, and you must have a birth certificate and a Social Security card. The military prefers enlistees, also called recruits, to have at least a high school diploma. Some branches require a college degree. Officers need a bachelor's or advanced degree. You must pass several physical and medical tests when you apply.

Once accepted you must go through basic training, which includes six to 11 weeks of courses in military life and protocol, as well as physical training. When basic training is com-

pleted, tests and interviews are used to assign recruits to work that matches their skills. Some recruits will be eligible for officer training programs, while others will be assigned to an enlisted position. Following basic training, most recruits take 10 to 20 weeks of technical training to prepare them for their assigned jobs. Enlisted personnel sign a contract, which commits them to eight years of service.

MILITARY BY THE NUMBERS

There are 1.2 million people employed in the armed forces. Here is the breakdown by branch:

Army	445,000
Navy	272,000
Air Force	343,000
Marine Corps	143,000
Coast Guard	26,000

More than one-third of military jobs are located in California, Texas, North Carolina, or Virginia. In 1998, 258,000 military personnel were stationed outside the United States, including those assigned to ships at sea.

Earnings

New military recruits earn from $11,500 to $14,200, depending on qualifications. Increases are scheduled on a regular basis, beginning four months after enlistment. The base compensation for enlisted personnel at the end of the first four-year tour of duty can be as much as $23,000 a year. Officers start at $22,000 to $31,000. The highest ranking officers with 20 years of service can earn $106,700 or more. Military personnel do not have to pay for their own housing, food, clothing, or medical care. They are eligible for a month's vacation each year, and receive retirement benefits after 20 years of service.

Outlook

The job outlook should be good in all branches of the armed forces through 2008. About 365,000 enlisted personnel and officers must be recruited each year to replace those who complete their commitment or retire.

FOR MORE INFO

Army Recruiting Command
Office of Information
Fort Sheridan, IL 60037
800-USA-ARMY
http://www.dtic.mil/armylink

Marine Corps Recruiting Command
3280 Russell Road
Quantico, VA 22134-5103
703-784-9433
http://www.mcrc.usmc.mil

Navy Recruiting Command
801 North Randolph Street
Arlington, VA 32203
800-USA-NAVY
http://www.navy.com

USAF Recruiting Command
Randolph Air Force Base
550 D Street West, Suite 1
San Antonio, TX 78150
210-652-3104
http://www.airforce.com

**U.S. Coast Guard
Information Center**
14180 Dallas Parkway, Suite 326
Dallas, TX 75240-9795
800-GET-USCG
http://www.dot.gov/dotinfo/uscg

Park Rangers

What Park Rangers Do

Park rangers protect animals and preserve forests, ponds, and other natural resources in state and national parks. They teach visitors about the park by giving lectures and tours. They also enforce rules and regulations to maintain a safe environment for visitors and wildlife.

One of the most important responsibilities park rangers have is safety. Rangers often require visitors to register at park offices so they will know when the visitors are expected to return from a hike or other activity. Rangers are trained in first aid and, if there is an accident, they may have to help visitors who have been injured. Rangers carefully mark hiking trails and other areas to lessen the risk of injuries for visitors and to protect plants and animals.

Rangers help visitors enjoy and learn about parks. They give lectures and provide guided tours of the park, explaining the park. Then they develop plans to help reduce pollution to make the park a better place for plants, animals, and visitors.

Rangers also do bookkeeping and other paperwork. They issue permits to visitors and keep track of how many people use the park. They also plan recreational activities and decide how to spend the money budgeted to the park.

Many accidents occur in national parks. For that reason, rangers must be trained in first aid and emergency care.

why certain plants and animals live there. They explain about the rocks and soil in the area and point out important historical sites.

Research and conservation efforts are also a big part of a park ranger's responsibilities. They study wildlife behavior by tagging and following certain animals. They may investigate sources of pollution that come from outside

EXPLORING

• You may be able to volunteer at national, state, or county parks. Universities and conservation organizations often have volunteer groups that work on research activities, studies, and rehabilitation efforts.

• Get to know your local wildlife. What kind of insects, birds, fish, and other animals live in your area? Your librarian will be able to help you find books that identify local flora and fauna.

PARKS IN DANGER

The National Parks Conservation Association listed the 10 most endangered national parks in 2000. The names of the parks are followed by their major threats.

Yellowstone National Park: Snowmobiles, which cause noise, ground, and air pollution.

Denali National Park: Proposal to open access by snowmobiles. Road and resort development.

Joshua Tree National Park: Proposed landfill site 1.5 miles outside the park.

Haleakala National Park: Introduction of non-native organisms that threaten rare plants and animals.

Everglades and Biscayne National Parks, and Big Cypress National Preserve: Damage from water management. Off-road vehicle use. Proposed airport development.

Petrified Forest National Park: Visitors taking an estimated 12 tons of fossilized wood annually.

Stones River National Battlefield: Proposed highway and commercial development.

National Underground Railroad Network to Freedom: Lack of funding for buying private property needed for the preservation of this network of sites.

Great Smoky Mountains National Park: Air pollution from regional power-generating plants and motor vehicles.

Ozarks Scenic Riverways National Park: Mining in the surrounding Mark Twain National Forest.

Education and Training

Park rangers usually have bachelor's degrees in natural resource or recreational resource management. A degree in many other fields is also acceptable, such as biology or ecology. Classes in forestry, geology, outdoor management, history, geography, behavioral sciences, and botany are helpful.

Without a degree, you need at least three years of experience working in parks or conservation. You must know about protecting plants and animals and enjoy working outdoors. You also need a pleasant personality and the ability to work with many different kinds of people. You should be good at explaining the natural environment and be able to enforce park rules and regulations. Rangers do receive some on-the-job training.

Earnings

Rangers in the National Park Service usually earn starting salaries of around $22,000 a year. More experienced or educated rangers earn approximately $33,000 a year. The government may provide housing to park rangers who work in remote areas.

Outlook

The number of people who want to become park rangers has always been far greater than the number of positions available. The National Park Service has reported that as many as 100 people apply for each job opening. This trend should continue into the future, and because of this stiff compe-

FOR MORE INFO

Contact the following groups for more information on a career as a park ranger:

National Parks Conservation Association
1300 19th Street, NW, Suite 300
Washington, DC 20036
202-223-6722
http://www.npca.org/

National Recreation and Park Association
22377 Belmont Ridge Road
Ashburn, VA 20148-4510
703-858-0784
http://www.nrpa.org

Student Conservation Association
PO Box 550
Charlestown, NH 03603-0550
603-543-1700
http://www.sca-inc.org

tition for positions, the job outlook is expected to change little. Besides the National Park Service, there are some job opportunities in other federal land and resource management agencies and similar state and local agencies.

Parole Officers

The Parole System Begins

Although aspects of parole were tried as early as 1817 in New York State, a complete system of conditional and early release did not begin in the United States until the 1870s. The new program, begun in New York, included a method of grading prisoners, compulsory education, and supervision by volunteers called guardians, with whom a released prisoner was required to meet periodically. By 1916, every state and the District of Columbia had established a similar program. This system of early release from prison came to be called parole—French for promise, or speech—because prisoners were freed on their word, or parole, of honor.

What Parole Officers Do

People who are on parole, called parolees, have been released from correctional institutions after serving part of a sentence as punishment for a crime. *Parole officers* supervise them after their release. Parole officers usually first meet parolees in prison, to explain the conditions of their release. Sometimes parole officers also help prisoners appearing before a parole board to prepare a case for their release.

Parolees are released from prison to make a new start and overcome their previous problems. Parole officers help them find a place to live and a new job. They also give advice and emotional support. Sometimes parolees need special help, so an officer may refer them to a counselor or clinic.

Probation officers are similar to parole officers. They supervise offenders who, instead of going to prison, are sentenced to a set amount of time during which they must check in regularly with their officers and follow certain restrictions on their activities.

Parole officers check frequently on parolees to make sure they obey the conditions of their release. Conditions might include attending school or a treatment program, abstaining from drug or alcohol use, and doing community service. Officers also talk to parolees' employers or teachers, family, and friends. They keep records for the courts, which include information about parolees' physical and mental health, finances, family, and social activities. Some parole officers are assigned to children or juveniles who have committed crimes. These officers investigate the conditions of a child's home, talk with parents and teachers, and work with other social workers assigned to the child.

If a parolee commits further crimes or does not obey the terms of release, a parole officer begins procedures to return the parolee to a correctional institution. Officers in some states arrest troublesome parolees. Working with parolees is sometimes dangerous.

EXPLORING

• There may be a church or community group in your area that has a program for helping rehabilitate parolees. You may try contacting them to see if there are volunteer opportunities.

• Here are some reading suggestions:

Capital Punishment: Crime, Justice, and Punishment by Robert V. Wolf (Chelsea House Publishers, 1997).

Crime and Punishment: Changing Attitudes 1900-2000 by Alison Brownlie (Raintree Stech-Vaughn Publishers, 1999).

Making Good: How Ex-Convicts Reform and Rebuild Their Lives by Shadd Maruma and Hans Toch (American Psychological Association, 2000).

Keeping Ex-Offenders Free!: An Aftercare Guide by Donald Smarto (Baker Books, 1993).

Education and Training

To prepare for a career as a parole officer, concentrate on English and social science classes. When you get to high school, take classes in civics, government, and psychology. Learning a foreign language will also be helpful.

Parole officers must have a bachelor's degree in criminal justice, social work, psychology, law, or another related field. Government agencies require a master's degree and experience in social work.

Earnings

Starting salaries for parole officers range from about $20,000 to $28,000 a year. The average annual salary ranges from $25,000 to $35,000. Parole officers who work for the federal government receive the highest salaries, with an average of $41,000 a year. Educational

1999 PAROLE FACTS

- A record 3,773,600 people were on parole in the United States and 712,700 were on probation.

- States with the largest percentages of their adult populations under community supervision were Georgia, with 5.8 percent, and Idaho, with 4.2 percent.

- More than 1 million of the nation's probationers and parolees lived in Texas and California.

- More than 1.9 million probationers and 400,000 parolees were discharged from supervision.

- Fourteen percent of probationers and 42 percent of parolees leaving supervision were incarcerated because of a rule violation or new offense.

- Twenty-two percent of probationers and 12 percent of parolees were women.

- Fifteen states had abolished their parole boards, confining criminals until they have served their full sentences.

level also affects salary. Parole officers with advanced degrees generally earn more than those with bachelor's degrees.

Outlook

The employment outlook for parole officers is good through the year 2008, according to the U.S. Department of Labor. The number of prisoners increased dramatically during the past decade and many of these will become eligible for parole. Overcrowding of prisons, combined with the high cost of keeping someone in jail, will lead to the early release of many convicts who will require supervision. However, public outcry over leniency toward convicted criminals, particularly repeat offenders, has created demand and even legislation for stiffer penalties and the withdrawal of the possibility of parole for many crimes. This development may ultimately decrease the demand for parole officers, as more and more criminals serve their full sentences.

FOR MORE INFO

For a list of accredited bachelor's and master's degree programs in social work, contact:
Council on Social Work Education
1725 Duke Street, Suite 500
Alexandria, VA 22314
703-683-8080
http://www.cswe.org/

For information on careers in social work, contact:
National Association of Social Workers
750 First Street, NE, Suite 700
Washington, DC 20002-4241
202-408-8600
http://www.naswdc.org/

Contact the ACA for information on job openings and for a list of colleges that offer degree programs in corrections:
The American Correctional Association
4380 Forbes Boulevard
Lanham, MD 20706-4322
800-222-5646
http://www.corrections.com/aca

RELATED JOBS

Corrections Officers
Human Services Workers
Lawyers and Judges
Police Officers
Psychologists
Social Workers

Police Officers

Words to Learn

Adam codes:
Radio codes used to describe types of calls. For example, A1 means arrest, A20 means assistance rendered, and A63 means pursuit.

Probable cause:
Information uncovered by officers that gives them a reason to arrest, search, or stop and detain a person.

Reasonable suspicion:
The reasons an officer believes a person should be stopped and detained.

What Police Officers Do

Police officers protect the lives and property of citizens by upholding and enforcing laws. Police officers preserve the peace, prevent criminal acts, and arrest people who break the law.

Some officers are assigned to traffic duties. They direct traffic during busy times of the day and ticket motorists who break traffic laws. Other police officers are assigned to patrol duties. These officers work in public places, such as in parks or on the streets, to make sure no one violates the law. They may patrol on foot, in squad cars, on bicycles, on motorcycles, or on horseback. They also look out for stolen cars, missing children, and persons wanted by law enforcement agencies.

Police officers also help in emergency situations. They administer first aid to accident victims, see that sick or injured people are rushed to hospitals, and help firefighters by controlling crowds and rerouting traffic. Police officers also prevent or break up violent disturbances.

Most police officers are trained to use firearms and carry guns. Police in special divisions, such as chemical analysis and handwriting and fingerprint identification, have special training. Officers often testify in court regarding the cases they handle. Police also have to complete accurate and thorough records of their cases.

Education and Training

The requirements for becoming a police officer are strict. You must pass many tests to prove you are qualified to be a police officer. These tests include written exams and tests of physical strength, dexterity, and endurance. Medical histories are checked carefully to find any medical condition that might hinder your work. There are background checks to make sure you are a U.S. citizen and have no history of criminal activity or convictions.

Most police departments require you to have at least a high school education. In some cases, you need college training. Many colleges and junior colleges now offer programs in law enforcement, police work, and police administration.

EXPLORING

• Many police departments have programs for kids. Look for educational events that teach you about street safety, Internet safety, or self-defense.

• Participate in police-sponsored sports events or social activities. It will give you a chance to meet and talk with police officers.

• Play games and make up exercises to test your memory and powers of observation. For example, you might play a video you have never seen before. Forward the tape to a random spot and play it for 30 seconds. Stop the video and write down everything you observed. Describe the setting, the people, their clothing, what they said, background noise, and so on. Then replay the video and check your accuracy. Try this with friends and compare notes.

After you are accepted by a police force, you start special training. It may last from three to six months or longer. Training usually includes classroom work in local, state, and federal laws; physical fitness training; firearm instruction; and legal procedures for enforcing the law.

Earnings

According to the U.S. Department of Labor, police officers in 1998 earned annual average salaries of $37,700. Salaries ranged from less than $19,200 a year to more than $63,500 a year. Police officers in supervisory positions earned about $48,700 a year in 1998, although earnings ranged from $28,700 to more than $84,700. Sheriffs and other law enforcement officers earned median annual salaries of $26,700 in 1998.

Salaries for police officers range widely based on location. Police departments in the West and North generally pay more than those in the South.

Outlook

Jobs for police officers will increase faster than the average through 2008. There is a lot of competition for openings. This occupation has a very low turnover rate. However, new positions will open as officers retire, leave the force, or move into higher positions. Police officers retire early compared to other occupations. Many retire while in their 40s and then pursue second careers.

In the past 10 years, private security firms have taken over some police activities, such as patrolling airports and other public places. Some private companies even provide police forces for entire cities. Many companies and universities also operate their own police forces.

FOR MORE INFO

American Police Academy
1000 Connecticut Avenue, NW, Suite 9
Washington, DC 20036
202-293-9088

National Police Officers Association of America
PO Box 22129
Louisville, KY 40252-0129
800-467-6762

National United Law Enforcement Officers Association
256 East McLemore Avenue
Memphis, TN 38106
800-533-4649

RELATED JOBS

Bodyguards
Border Patrol Officers
Corrections Officers
Crime Analysts
Cryptographic Technicians
Deputy U.S. Marshals
Detectives
FBI Agents
Intelligence Officers
Parole Officers

Regional and Local Officials

The Evolution of Local Government

The first U.S. colonies adopted the English "shire" form of government. This form came from medieval England, where a county was overseen by a sheriff (originally a "shire reeve") appointed by the crown and was represented by two members in Parliament. The "shire" form served as the administrative arm of both the national and local governments in early America.

When America's founding fathers composed the Constitution, they didn't make any specific provisions for the governing of cities and counties. This allowed state governments to draw up their own constitutions.

City and county governments strengthened during the 19th century, especially after World War II, due to population growth, rising revenues, and increased independence from the states.

What Regional and Local Officials Do

Regional and local officials include mayors, commissioners, and city and county council members. These officials are elected or appointed to direct regional legal services, public health departments, and police and fire protection. They deal with water quality, housing, public health, and budget and financial management. They attend meetings and serve on committees that address specific problems and try to find a solution. They vote on laws, and generally represent the people in their districts.

There are two forms of county government. In the commissioner-administrator form, a county board of commissioners appoints an administrator who makes sure the board's policies are carried out. In the council-executive form, a county executive is the chief administrative officer of the district and has the power to veto laws and regulations passed by the county board. A county government may include a chief executive, who directs regional services; council members, who are the county legislators; a county clerk, who keeps records of property titles, licenses, etc.; and a county treasurer who is in charge of the receipt and disbursement of money.

City, or municipal, governments also have different forms. In mayor-council governments, a mayor and city council members are elected. The council is responsible for formulating city ordinances, but the mayor has control over the actions of the council. In a commission government, the people elect a number of commissioners, each of whom serves as head of a city department. The presiding commissioner is usually the mayor. Another type of municipal government is the council-manager form. Council members are elected by the people, and the council hires a city manager to administer the city departments. A mayor is elected by the council to chair the council and officiate at important municipal functions.

Education and Training

To serve on a local government, your experience and understanding of the city or county are generally more important

EXPLORING

• Visit your county courthouse or city hall. Most conduct tours for the public.

• Volunteer to work for county-organized programs, such as tutoring in a literacy program or leading children's reading groups at the public library.

• Become involved with local elections. Many candidates for local and state offices welcome young people to assist with campaigns by making calls, posting signs, and handing out brochures and flyers.

• Become involved in local issues that interest you. Maybe there's an old building in your neighborhood you'd like to save from destruction, or maybe you have some ideas for youth programs or programs for senior citizens. Research what's being done about your concerns and come up with solutions to offer local officials.

MODEL COUNTY PROGRAMS

The National Association of Counties (NACO) sponsors achievement awards that recognize innovative government programs and projects in such areas as arts and historic preservation, children and youth, and employment and training. Here are a few of NACO's "County Model Programs":

- Students in the local schools of Jane City, Virginia, were invited to draw an ideal playground. Volunteers and donations were then sought by the Parks and Recreation Department, and "Kidsburg" was built from these student designs.
- Johnson County, Kansas, introduced a program to bring more older volunteers into public schools for tutoring and for speaking to students in the Living History Program, which features stories of the past.
- After Hurricane Andrew, many lost pets could not be returned to their owners because of loss of identification and lack of communication among humane organizations. In response, Orange County, Florida, has developed disaster planning kits and new animal shelters in the event of future natural disasters.

than your educational background. Some mayors and council members are elected into their positions because they've lived in the region for a long time and have had experience with local business, industry, and other concerns. For example, someone with years of experience with farming in the region may be the best candidate to serve for a small agricultural community. Voters in local elections may be more impressed by a candidate's previous occupations and roles in the community than they are by a candidate's postsecondary degrees.

To serve as an executive or council member for a large city or county, however, you are likely to need an undergraduate degree. Officials have degrees in such areas as public administration, law, economics, political science, and history.

Earnings

In general, salaries for government officials tend to be lower than what those officials could make working in the private sector. In many local offices, officials volunteer their time or work only part-time. According to a 1998 salary survey by the International City/County Management Association, the chief elected official of a city makes an average salary of $12,870 a year. The average salary for city managers was $70,500 in 1997. A county's chief elected official averages $26,420 a year. County clerks make about $38,000, while treasurers earn $36,000, and chief law enforcement officials earn $48,000 a year.

Outlook

Every election, voters decide whether to keep their current forms of government or to introduce new forms. But these changes don't greatly affect the

FOR MORE INFO

National Association of Counties
440 First Street, NW
Washington, DC 20001
202-393-6226
http://www.naco.org

International City/County Management Association
777 North Capitol Street, NE, Suite 500
Washington, DC 20002
202-289-4262
http://www.icma.org

number of officials needed to run local governments.

The issues facing a community will have the most effect on the jobs of local officials. Cities with older neighborhoods deal with historic preservation, improvements in utilities, and water quality. In a growing city with many suburbs, officials have to make decisions regarding development, roads, and expanded routes for public transportation.

Secret Service Special Agents

What Secret Service Special Agents Do

Secret Service special agents protect U.S. leaders or foreign leaders who are visiting the United States. Special agents also investigate the counterfeiting of U.S. currency. Special agents can carry and use firearms, execute warrants, and make arrests.

Special agents plan the best ways to guard the people they are assigned to protect. For example, an advance team of special agents surveys the places a protectee (see the sidebar, Words to Learn) is scheduled to visit. They identify hospitals and exit routes and work closely with local police, fire, and rescue units to develop a protection plan. They set up a command post as the communication center for protective activities. Before the protectee arrives, a lead advance agent coordinates all law enforcement representatives participating in the visit. He or she tells agents where they will be posted and notifies them about any special concerns. Just before the arrival of the protectee, agents set up checkpoints and limit access to the secure area. After the visit, special agents analyze every step of the operation, record unusual incidents, and suggest improvements for the future.

When secret service special agents are not working on a protective assignment, they work on crime investigations. For example, they investigate threats made to protectees and cases of counterfeit currency, forgery, and financial crimes.

Education and Training

Computer and foreign language classes are good preparation for a career in the Secret Service, as are government and English classes.

After high school there are several ways to qualify for entry into the Secret Service. You can earn a four-year degree from a college or university. You can work for at least three years in a criminal investigative or law enforcement field. Or a combination of education and experience can also qualify you.

All newly hired agents go through nine weeks of training at the Federal Law

EXPLORING

• Visit the Kids Only page on the Secret Service Web site at http://www.treas.gov/usss.

• The Secret Service offers the Stay-In-School Program for high school students. The program allows students who meet financial eligibility guidelines to earn money by working for the agency part-time, usually in a clerical job.

THEN AND NOW

The Secret Service was established in 1865 to stop the counterfeiting of U.S. currency. After the assassination of President William McKinley in 1901, the Secret Service was directed by Congress to protect the president of the United States. Today it is the Secret Service's responsibility to protect the following people:

- The president and vice president (also president-elect and vice president-elect) and their immediate families

- Former presidents and their spouses for 10 years after the president leaves office (spouses lose protection if they remarry)

- Children of former presidents until they are 16 years old

- Visiting heads of foreign states or governments and their spouses traveling with them, along with other distinguished foreign visitors to the United States and their spouses traveling with them

- Official representatives of the United States who are performing special missions abroad

- Major presidential and vice-presidential candidates and, within 120 days of the general presidential election, their spouses

Enforcement Training Center in Glynco, Georgia. This is followed by 11 weeks of specialized training at the Secret Service's Training Academy in Beltsville, Maryland.

Special agents must be U.S. citizens; be at least 21 at the time of appointment; have uncorrected vision no worse than 20/60 in each eye, correctable to 20/20 in each eye; pass the Treasury

Enforcement Agent exam; and undergo a complete background investigation, including in-depth interviews, drug screening, medical examination, and polygraph examination.

Earnings

Special agents usually start at an annual wage of $21,900 or $27,100. Agents automatically advance to higher levels each year until they reach the annual salary of $48,200. After that they compete for higher positions, which pay $57,300. The top Senior Executive Service salary in 1999 was $151,800.

Outlook

Compared to other federal law enforcement agencies, the Secret Service is small. Since the Secret Service employs a small number of people, their new hires each year are limited. The agency anticipated hiring about another 100 special agents in 1998. The number of job opportunities will remain about the same in the next 10 years.

FOR MORE INFO

Your local Secret Service field office or the personnel office at the following address, can provide more information on becoming a special agent. If you are writing about the Stay-In-School program, mark the envelope "Attention: Stay-In-School Program."
U.S. Secret Service
Personnel Division
950 H Street, NW, Room 912
Washington, DC 20001
202-406-5800
http://www.treas.gov/usss

RELATED JOBS

Bodyguards
Deputy U.S. Marshals
Detectives
FBI Agents
Intelligence Officers
Police Officers
Security Consultants and Technicians

Social Workers

What Do Those Letters Mean?

Social workers sometimes have a string of letters after their names. Some are abbreviations for academic degrees and others are abbreviations for different types of certification or credentials. Here's a decoder:

Academic Degrees
BSW: Bachelor of Social Work
MSW: Master of Social Work
MSSW: Master of Science in Social Work
MSS: Master of Social Science

Certification/Credentials
ACSW: Academy of Certified Social Workers
LCSW: Licensed Clinical Social Worker
QCSW: Qualified Clinical Social Worker
DCSW: Diplomate in Clinical Social Work

What Social Workers Do

Social workers help people with personal and community problems caused by poverty, homelessness, unemployment, illness, broken homes, family conflict, or physical, developmental, and emotional disabilities.

Most social workers meet face to face with troubled individuals or families. They work in schools to help students who have behavioral problems. They work in hospitals, helping sick people and their families adjust to the special problems caused by certain illnesses. They work in courts, police departments, and prison systems, counseling convicts, helping juvenile offenders, or helping soon-to-be released prisoners return to life outside the jail. Social workers are employed by adoption agencies, drug and alcohol abuse programs, and agencies that help families find solutions to financial, emotional, or medical problems.

Social workers also work with groups and may be employed by community centers, settlement houses, youth organizations, institutions for children or the elderly, hospitals, prisons, or housing projects. They provide both rehabilitation and recreational activities for groups of people with similar handicaps or problems. Social workers might help migrant workers adjust to their temporary surroundings. They might hold workshops for parents of diabetic children or for the children themselves. They also might work in nursing homes, planning social and recreational activities for the elderly.

Social workers who work for community organizations try to analyze the problems of an entire community and find ways to solve these problems. Juvenile delinquency, high unemployment, and high crime rates are other such problems that might require total community cooperation for a solution.

Education and Training

Social workers must be sensitive to people's problems and be able to handle them with a concerned, caring attitude, even if the problems make the worker sad or angry. Social workers have to be able to accept responsibility and to try to

EXPLORING

• Volunteer at a social service agency or community organization.

• Work as a counselor in a camp for children with disabilities.

• Your local YMCA/ YWCA, park district, or other recreational facility may need volunteers for group recreation programs, including programs designed to prevent delinquency.

• Volunteer a few afternoons a week to read to people in retirement homes or to the blind.

• Work as a reporter for your school newspaper. You will have the opportunity to interview people, conduct surveys, and learn about social change, all of which are important aspects of the social work profession.

solve problems even if they are under pressure. To prepare for social work, you should take courses in high school that will improve your communication skills, such as English, speech, and composition. History, social studies, and sociology courses are important in understanding the concerns and issues of society.

A social worker must have a bachelor's degree in social work from an approved four-year college or university. Most students then complete at least 400 hours of supervised social work practice. Jobs with the most rewards and responsibilities go to applicants with a master's degree in social work (MSW). A doctorate is required for some teaching, research, and supervisory jobs. All states require licensing, certification, or registration of social workers.

PROFILE: JANE ADDAMS (1860-1935)

Jane Addams, social worker, reformer, and peace advocate, made Hull House in Chicago world-famous as a settlement house (social-welfare center). She shared the 1931 Nobel Peace Prize with Nicholas Murray Butler, president of Columbia University. She was elected to the Hall of Fame for Great Americans in 1965.

In 1889 Addams and Ellen Gates Starr, a college classmate, rented a decrepit mansion known as Hull House, located in one of Chicago's worst slums. Here Addams, Starr, and other volunteers held classes for immigrants, provided day care for babies, and operated a community center, dispensary, coffee shop, art gallery, theater, gymnasium, and cooperative boardinghouse for working women. Addams solicited financial support, had new buildings erected around Hull House, and recruited volunteer workers, mostly middle- and upper-class women. Hull House became a training center for social workers and a model for similar settlement houses in other parts of the United States.

Addams campaigned for political and social reforms, including women's suffrage, protection of working women, strict child labor laws, recognition of labor unions, improvements in public welfare, more playgrounds, and separate courts for juvenile offenders.

Earnings

The median salary for social workers in the United States was about $30,590 in 1998, according to the U.S. Department of Labor. Salaries ranged from $19,250 to $49,000. Social workers employed by the U.S. government earn an average annual salary of about $45,300.

Outlook

The field of social work is expected to grow much faster than the average for all occupations through 2008, according to the U.S. Department of Labor. The biggest reason for this growth is the increasing number of older people who need social services. Social workers who specialize in gerontology will find many job opportunities in nursing homes, hospitals, and home health care agencies.

Schools will also need more social workers to deal with issues such as teenage pregnancies and integration of students with disabilities into the

FOR MORE INFO

For information on social work careers and educational programs, contact:
Council on Social Work Education
1725 Duke Street, Suite 500
Alexandria, VA 22314
703-683-8080
http://www.cswe.org

Visit the NASW Web site to access the online publication, Choices: Careers in Social Work.
National Association of Social Workers
750 First Street, NE, Suite 700
Washington DC 20002-4241
202-408-8600
http://www.socialworkers.org

Canadian Association of Social Workers
383 Parkdale Avenue, Suite 402
Ottawa, Ontario Canada K1Y 4R4
613-729-6668
http://www.intranet.ca/-casw

general school population. There is also a growing number of people with illnesses and physical disabilities or impairments staying in their own homes, and they will need social workers to arrange for home health care services.

Spies

What Spies Do

Spies, also called *intelligence officers,* work for the U.S. government to gather information about the governments of foreign countries. This information, called *intelligence,* is one of the tools the U.S. government uses to help make decisions about its own military, economic, and political policies. Intelligence may include political, economic, military, scientific, technical, geographic, and other types of information, both public and secret.

There are two types of intelligence officers, case officers and analysts. *Case officers,* also called *operators,* are most often involved in the colorful and dangerous sorts of activities shown in the movies. They collect intelligence, usually in foreign countries. They contact people who supply them with the valuable information they need. *Analysts* are more likely to be stationed in an office in Washington, D.C., although some also work abroad.

What Is Intelligence?

Intelligence is information gathered by intelligence officers to help the U.S. government and its policy makers. There are several different kinds of intelligence:

Current intelligence is information about day-to-day events.

Estimative intelligence considers what might be or what might happen.

Warning intelligence gives notice to policy makers that something urgent might happen that may require their immediate attention.

Research intelligence is an in-depth study of an issue.

Scientific and technical intelligence is information on foreign technologies.

They interpret and analyze data they have received from case officers and other sources. *Technical analysts* gather data from satellites. *Cryptographic technicians* are experts at encoding, decoding, and sending secret messages.

There are three categories of intelligence operations: strategic, tactical, and counter-intelligence. People working in *strategic intelligence* keep track of world events, watch foreign leaders very carefully, and study a foreign country's politics, economy, its people, its military status, and any scientific advances it may be making. *Tactical intelligence-gathering* involves collecting the same kind of information, but in combat areas and risky political settings abroad. *Counter-intelligence officers* protect U.S. secrets, institutions, and intelligence activities. They identify and prevent enemy operations that might hurt the United States, its citizens, or its allies. Such enemy plots include worldwide terrorism and drug trafficking.

Education and Training

All of the federal intelligence services are looking for people of high moral character, excellent academic records, and sincere patriotic commitment. Applicants

EXPLORING

Here are some books, movies, and a Web site to explore.

Books
The Spy Who Came In from the Sea by Peggy Nolan (Pineapple Press, 1999).

Spies and Traitors by Stewart Ross (Copper Beach Books, 1995).

In the Line of Fire: Eight Women War Spies by George Sullivan (Scholastic Paperbacks, 1996).

Movies
Tinker, Tailor, Soldier, Spy directed by John Irvin (1980).

The 39 Steps directed by Alfred Hitchcock (1935).

Above Suspicion directed by Richard Thorpe (1943).

Web Site
CIA Kids Home Page
http://www.odci.gov/cia/ciakids/index.html

FAMOUS WOMEN SPIES

Lydia Barrington Darragh spied on the British during the American Revolution and informed American officers.

Sarah Bradlee Fulton, called the "mother of the Boston Tea Party" delivered messages through enemy lines.

Belle Boyd spied for the Confederacy and carried letters and papers across enemy lines during the Civil War.

Elizabeth Van Lew spied for the North during the Civil War, setting up a network of couriers and inventing a code.

Edith Cavell, a nurse from England, helped British, French, and Belgian soldiers escape from behind German lines during WW I.

Virginia Hall worked for the French as an agent and later for America's OSS (Office of Strategic Services) during WW II, successfully evading the Nazis.

must be U.S. citizens and at least 21 years old. You must earn a bachelor's degree, and an advanced degree for some positions. Specialized skills, computer knowledge, and fluency in foreign languages are also important.

Candidates for field operations need to feel comfortable in social situations, make friends easily, and enjoy risk. They have to be able to think quickly. Candidates for analyst positions usually have advanced degrees, are more studious, and are more comfortable working in an office.

Earnings

The starting salary for intelligence officers with a bachelor's degree ranges from $25,500 to $37,700. A candidate with an advanced degree in engineering or a physical science may start as high as $50,000. Those with experience and knowledge of a foreign language also earn higher salaries. Those in top management earn from $67,000 to $90,000 a year. Officers who work abroad receive free housing and allowances and benefits. Those employed in secret or hazardous operations also receive higher pay.

Outlook

The decline of communism in Eastern Europe and the former Soviet republics means that this major threat has been greatly reduced. However, there are ongoing threats of terrorism from other parts of the world, so the need for intelligence activities will remain high. Intelligence agencies are concerned with the spread of nuclear, chemical, and biological weapons, as well as threats from foreign nuclear reactors and nuclear waste to the environment, natural resources, and worldwide human health.

U.S. News & World Report reported in 1998 that the CIA was actively searching for new

recruits, especially among women and minorities. They were particularly interested in hiring computer scientists, engineers, and fluent speakers of Chinese and Arabic.

FOR MORE INFO

For further information, contact:
**CIA Employment and
Recruitment Center**
PO Box 12727
Arlington, VA 22209-8727
http://www.odci.gov/cia/employment/ciaeindex.htm

Defense Intelligence Agency
200 MacDill Boulevard
Civilian Personnel Division (DAH-2)
Washington, DC 20340-5100
http://www.dia.mil

RELATED JOBS

Crime Analysts
Cryptographic Technicians
Detectives
FBI Agents
Security Consultants and Technicians

State and Federal Officials

Did You Know?

The United States Constitution requires that a U.S. senator be at least 30 years of age, a citizen of the United States for at least nine years, and a resident of the state from which he or she is chosen.

Each state's two senators serve six-year terms. Representatives serve two-year terms.

The Constitution assigns the Senate and House equal responsibility for declaring war, maintaining the armed forces, assessing taxes, borrowing money, minting currency, regulating commerce, and making all laws necessary for the operation of the government. The Senate holds exclusive authority to advise and consent on treaties and nominations.

What State and Federal Officials Do

State and federal officials include governors, judges, senators, representatives, and the president and vice president of the country. Government officials protect the government against external and domestic threats, supervise and resolve conflicts between private and public interests, regulate the economy, protect political and social rights of citizens, and provide goods and services. Officials may, among other things, pass laws, set up social service programs, and decide how the taxpayers' money should be spent for goods and services, such as welfare and education.

The executive branch of the government includes the *president* and *vice president* who are elected by voters. Other officials include members of the president's Cabinet: the secretaries of state, treasury, defense, interior, agriculture, and health and human services. These officials are appointed by the president and approved by the Senate. The members of the Office of Management and Budget, the Council of Economic Advisors, and the National Security Council are also executive officers of the national government.

State governments are headed by governors and lieutenant governors. The *governor* is the chief executive officer of a state and manages the state's agriculture, highway and motor-vehicle departments, public safety and corrections, regulation of intrastate business and industry, and some aspects of education, public health, and welfare. Some states also have a *lieutenant governor,* who serves as the presiding officer of the state's senate. Other elected state officials commonly include a *secretary of state, state treasurer, state auditor, attorney general,* and *superintendent of public instruction.*

State *senators* and state *representatives* are the legislators elected to represent each state's districts and regions of cities and counties in the U.S. Congress. In the U.S. Congress, there are 100 senators and 435 representatives. The primary function of all legislators is to make laws. Senators and representatives research legislation, prepare reports, meet with con-

EXPLORING

• Become involved in student government at your school.

• Volunteer to help with local election campaigns. You can make calls, post signs, and distribute literature. Volunteering gives you an opportunity to meet candidates and others with an interest in government.

• Read about the bills up for vote in the state legislature and U.S. Congress.

• Visit the Web sites of the House and Senate and of your state legislature to read about bills, schedules, and the legislators. The National Conference of State Legislators also hosts a Web site. (See For More Info.)

stituents and interest groups, speak to the press, and discuss legislation in the House or Senate. Legislators also may be involved in activities like selecting other members of the government, supervising the government administration, appropriating funds, and determining election procedures.

Education and Training

State and federal legislators come from all walks of life. Some hold master's degrees and doctorates, while others have only a high school education. The majority of government officials hold law degrees, but some have undergraduate or graduate degrees in journalism, economics, political science, history, public administration, or international affairs.

Experience is important for state and federal officials. They often begin at the local level of government.

Earnings

The U.S. Department of Labor reports that the median annual earnings of government chief executives and legislators were $19,130 in 1998. Salaries generally ranged from less than $11,460 to more than $81,230, although some officials earn nothing at all and the president earns $400,000 annually.

According to the National Conference of State Legislators, state legislators earn from $10,000 to $47,000 a year. A few states, however, don't pay state legislators anything but an expense allowance. The *Book*

WHO REPRESENTS YOU?

To find the elected officials who represent you in government, go to this Web site and type in your zip code: http://government.aol.com.

of the States lists salaries of state governors as ranging from $60,000 in Arkansas to a high of $130,000 in New York.

In 2001, U.S. senators and representatives earned $145,100, the Senate and House Majority and Minority Leaders earned $161,200, and the vice president earned $186,300. Congressional leaders such as the Speaker of the House and the Senate Majority Leader receive higher salaries than the other Congress members. The Speaker of the House earns $186,300 a year.

Outlook

Little or no change is expected in the employment of federal and state officials through 2008. An increase in the number of representatives is possible as the U.S. population grows, but would require additional office space and other costly expansions. For the most part, the structures of state and federal legislatures will remain unchanged. The topic of limiting the number of terms that a representative is allowed to serve often arises in election years.

FOR MORE INFO

Visit the Senate and House Web sites for information about Congress, government history, and current legislation. The site also provides links to the sites of state legislatures. To ask about internship opportunities with your Congress member, contact his or her office at:
U.S. Senate
Office of Senator (Name)
United States Senate
Washington, DC 20515
202-224-3121
http://www.senate.gov

U.S. House of Representatives
Washington, DC 20515
202-224-3121
http://www.house.gov

For information about State Legislatures Magazine, *and other information concerning state legislatures, contact:*
National Conference of State Legislatures
444 North Capitol Street, NW, Suite 515
Washington, DC 20001
202-624-5400
http://www.ncsl.org

Glossary

accredited: Approved as meeting established standards for providing good training and education. This approval is usually given by an independent organization of professionals to a school or a program in a school. Compare **certified** and **licensed**.

apprentice: A person who is learning a trade by working under the supervision of a skilled worker. Apprentices often receive classroom instruction in addition to their supervised practical experience.

apprenticeship: 1. A program for training apprentices (see apprentice). 2. The period of time when a person is an apprentice. In highly skilled trades, apprenticeships may last three or four years.

associate's degree: An academic rank or title granted by a community or junior college or similar institution to graduates of a two-year program of education beyond high school.

bachelor's degree: An academic rank or title given to a person who has completed a four-year program of study at a college or university. Also called an undergraduate degree or baccalaureate.

certified: Approved as meeting established requirements for skill, knowledge, and experience in a particular field. People are certified by the organization of professionals in their field. Compare **accredited** and **licensed**.

community college: A public two-year college, attended by students who do not live at the college. Graduates of a community college receive an associate degree and may transfer to a four-year college or university to complete a bachelor's degree. Compare **junior college** and **technical college**.

diploma: A certificate or document given by a school to show that a person has completed a course or has graduated from the school.

doctorate: An academic rank or title (the highest) granted by a graduate school to a person who has completed a two- to three-year program after having received a master's degree.

fringe benefit: A payment or benefit to an employee in addition to regular wages or salary. Examples of fringe benefits include a pension, a paid vacation, and health or life insurance.

graduate school: A school that people may attend after they have received their bachelor's degree. People who complete an educational program at a graduate school earn a master's degree or a doctorate.

intern: An advanced student (usually one with at least some college training) in a professional field who is employed in a job that is intended to provide supervised practical experience for the student.

internship: 1. The position or job of an intern (see intern). 2. The period of time when a person is an intern.

junior college: A two-year college that offers courses like those in the first half of a four-year college program. Graduates of a junior college usually receive an associate degree and may transfer to a four-year college or university to complete a bachelor's degree. Compare **community college.**

liberal arts: The subjects covered by college courses that develop broad general knowledge rather than specific occupational skills. The liberal arts are often considered to include philosophy, literature and the arts, history, language, and some courses in the social sciences and natural sciences.

licensed: Having formal permission from the proper authority to carry out an activity that would be illegal without that permission. For example, a person may be licensed to practice medicine or to drive a car. Compare **certified**.

major: (in college) The academic field in which a student specializes and receives a degree.

master's degree: An academic rank or title granted by a graduate school to a person who has completed a one- or two-year program after having received a bachelor's degree.

pension: An amount of money paid regularly by an employer to a former employee after he or she retires from working.

private: 1. Not owned or controlled by the government (such as private industry or a private employment agency). 2. Intended only for a particular person or group; not open to all (such as a private road or a private club).

public: 1. Provided or operated by the government (such as a public library). 2. Open and available to everyone (such as a public meeting).

regulatory: Having to do with the rules and laws for carrying out an activity. A regulatory agency, for example, is a government organization that sets up required procedures for how certain things should be done.

scholarship: A gift of money to a student to help the student pay for further education.

social studies: Courses of study (such as civics, geography, and history) that deal with how human societies work.

starting salary: Salary paid to a newly hired employee. The starting salary is usually a smaller amount than is paid to a more experienced worker.

technical college: A private or public college offering two- or four-year programs in technical subjects. Technical colleges offer courses in both general and technical subjects and award associate degrees and bachelor's degrees.

technician: A worker with specialized practical training in a mechanical or scientific subject who works under the supervision of scientists, engineers, or other professionals. Technicians typically receive two years of college-level education after high school.

technologist: A worker in a mechanical or scientific field with more training than a technician. Technologists typically must have between two and four years of college-level education after high school.

undergraduate: A student at a college or university who has not yet received a degree.

undergraduate degree: See **bachelor's degree**.

union: An organization whose members are workers in a particular industry or company. The union works to gain better wages, benefits, and working conditions for its members. Also called a labor union or trade union.

vocational school: A public or private school that offers training in one or more skills or trades. Compare **technical college**.

wage: Money that is paid in return for work done, especially money paid on the basis of the number of hours or days worked.

Index of Job Titles

administrative officers, 38
administrators, 66
agents, 30-33
agricultural inspectors, 42
ambassadors, **6-9**
analysts, 78, 80
attorney general, 83

biologists, 34, 36

case officers, 78
chief administrative officers, 66
chief of staff, 17
city managers, **10-13,** 67, 69
clerks, 50
commissioners, 67
computer scientists, 81
computer specialists, 51
congressional aides, **14-17**
consular officers, 39
cooks, 50
corrections officers, **18-21**
council members, 67-68
county clerks, 67, 69
county treasurer, 67
criminal investigators, 35
cryptographic technicians, 79
customs inspectors, 43, 45
customs officials, **22-25**
customs warehouse officers, 24

dentists, 50
deputy sheriffs, 19

deputy U.S. marshals, **26-29**
doctors, 50

electronics experts, 50
engineers, 34, 81
environmental health
    inspectors, 43
environmental protection
    specialists, 45

FBI agents, **30-33**
fish and game wardens, **34-37**
food and drug inspectors, 42
foreign service officers, 8, 9,
    38-41

government officials, 82-85
governors, 82, 83, 85

health and regulatory
    inspectors, **42-45**

intelligence officers, 78-81
investigators, 30

judges, 82

law enforcement agents, 34
law enforcement officers, 26
law enforcement officials, 69
legislative assistants, 17
legislative correspondents, 14
legislative directors, 17

legislators, 46, 49, 67, 83, 84

lieutenant governors, 83

lobbyists, 16, **46-49**

marshals, 26-29

mayor, 10, 67

mechanics, 50

military workers, **50-53**

occupational safety and health
    inspectors, 44, 45

office managers, 14

operators, 78

park rangers, **54-57**

parole officers, **58-61**

police officers, 19, **62-65**

political officers, 39

president, 7, 8, 82-84

press secretaries, 14

probation officers, 58

quality assurance
    inspectors, 45

rangers, 54-57

realty specialists, 34

refuge managers, 35

refuge officers, 34

refuge rangers, 34, 35

regional and local officials,
    66-69

representatives, 14-17, 82,
    83, 85

scientists, 51

secret service special agents,
    70-73

secretary of state, 7, 8, 82, 83

senate majority leader, 85

senators, 14-17, 82, 83, 85

sergeants, 20

social workers, **74-77**

speaker of the house, 85

special agents, 30, 33, 35, 37,
    70-73

spies, **78-81**

state and federal officials, **82-85**

state auditor, 83

state or district directors, 14

state treasurer, 83

superintendent of public
    instruction, 83

technical analysts, 79

technicians, 50

U.S. marshals, 26-29

vice president, 82, 85

wildlife conservationists, 34

wildlife inspectors, 34, 35

wildlife managers, 34

Government on the Web

Ben's Guide to U.S. Government for Kids
http://bensguide.gpo.gov

FedStats Kids' Pages
http://www.fedstats.gov/kids.html

FirstGov
http://www.firstgov.gov

The Great American Web Site
http://www.uncle-sam.com

Foreign Service
http://www.state.gov

State and Local Government on the Net
http://www.piperinfo.com/state/index.cfm

U.S. Senate
http://www.senate.gov

U.S. House of Representatives
http://www.house.gov

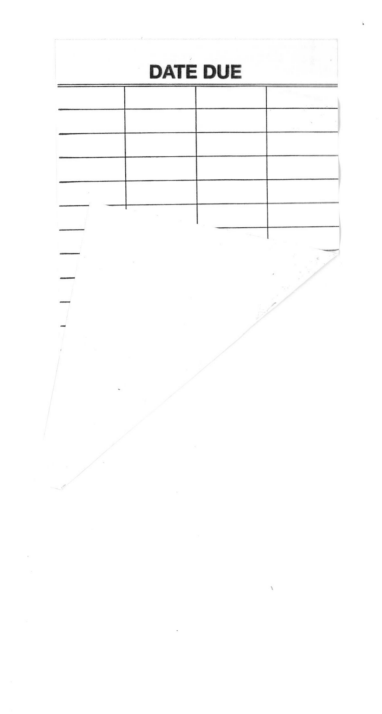

DATE DUE
